No Program but Time, No Book but the Bible

No Program but Time, No Book but the Bible

Reflections on Mentoring and Discipleship
in Honor of Scott M. Gibson

Edited by
Matthew D. Kim

Foreword by
Kenneth L. Swetland

Afterword by
Stephen Sebastian

WIPF & STOCK · Eugene, Oregon

NO PROGRAM BUT TIME, NO BOOK BUT THE BIBLE
Reflections on Mentoring and Discipleship in Honor of Scott M. Gibson

Copyright © 2018 Matthew D. Kim. All rights reserved. Except for brief quotations in critical publications or reviews, no part of this book may be reproduced in any manner without prior written permission from the publisher. Write: Permissions, Wipf and Stock Publishers, 199 W. 8th Ave., Suite 3, Eugene, OR 97401.

Wipf & Stock
An Imprint of Wipf and Stock Publishers
199 W. 8th Ave., Suite 3
Eugene, OR 97401

www.wipfandstock.com

PAPERBACK ISBN: 978-1-5326-4185-5
HARDCOVER ISBN: 978-1-5326-5285-1
EBOOK ISBN: 978-1-5326-5286-8

Manufactured in the U.S.A.

To Scott M. Gibson—

Thanks for investing in us.

Contents

Foreword by Kenneth L. Swetland | xi
Acknowledgments | xv
Introduction by Matthew D. Kim | xvii

Part One   Character

1. Cracks in My Character | 3
   Glen Massey

2. Contagious Character | 7
   Ken Shigematsu

Part Two   Hospitality

3. The Strange Power of Stranger-Love | 13
   John Meinen

4. Little Moments (Without Eggplant) | 17
   Tim A. Norton

5. Hospitality to Admire | 20
   Larry Torres

6. There's No Place Like Home for Discipleship | 23
   Jeff White

Part Three   Marriage and Family

7. Family | 29
   Earl Arnold

Contents

8. Mentorship: Adoption into Family Life | 34
   Benjamin C. Crelin

9. No Replacement for Family Time | 37
   Kyle Lincoln

10. Marriage, Family, and Mentors | 41
    Christopher H. Priestaf

Part Four   Mentoring and Discipleship

11. Three Principles of Mentorship | 47
    Chad Bryan

12. How Would Jesus Mentor? | 51
    Bill Haley

13. Three Pictures: One Image | 54
    Michael R. Mazzye

14. What Scott Gibson Taught Me About Discipleship | 57
    Derek Mondeau

Part Five   Pastoral Ministry

15. Wholeness in the Pastoral Call | 63
    Casey C. Barton

16. Being Present in Pastoral Ministry | 67
    Michael Curtis

17. The Fundamentals of Pastoral Ministry | 71
    Paul A. Hoffman

18. Pastoral Ministry: The Steadying Influence of a Godly Mentor | 75
    Dana J. Smith

Part Six   Preaching

19. Congregational Intent: The Questions of Your Congregation Are More Biblical Than You Think | 81
    Kerry L. Bender

20. Missional Preaching | 85
    Grant Buchholtz

Contents

21. Do What You Want: Getting to the Heart of Application | 89
    Eric Dokken
22. Discipling to the Task of Preaching | 93
    Nicholas Gatzke

Part Seven   Teaching and Academics

23. A Teacher of Teachers | 99
    Patricia Batten
24. Scott Gibson, the Teacher | 103
    Calvin W. Choi
25. Mentoring Millennials and Other Young Whippersnappers | 107
    Chris Rappazini
26. Advice for Applying for Grad School in Theology | 111
    Allen Yeh

Part Eight   Wisdom

27. Pastoral Wisdom | 119
    Thomas F. Backer
28. Well-Versed in Wisdom | 123
    John Q. Dao
29. The Fear of the Lord is the Beginning of Wisdom and True Fear of the Lord Comes through Discipleship | 125
    Chad D. Granger
30. Wisdom: The Right Path | 128
    Todd Regester
31. Wisdom's Pedagogy: Humility | 132
    Todd M. Smedley

Afterword: Living a Life of Mentoring Influence | 135
    Stephen Sebastian
Bibliography | 139

Foreword

Kenneth L. Swetland

The whole concept of mentoring as discipling has taken on heightened attention in the past several decades. Although discipling has always been a practice of God's people through the centuries, it has seen a renewed awakening in recent times—and has been a needed corrective in helping people mature in their faith as followers of Christ and leaders for the Church. The very word "mentor," however, has not been used as a synonym for discipling until recent times.

The word "mentor," of course, has been around for a long time and is fairly commonly used in various disciplines to describe someone who has experience and wisdom to pass along to a protégé, and who is somewhat detached from the person seeking counsel or advice. However, the word and practice have seen a marked increase in recent years.

When I entered graduate school nearly sixty years ago to begin academic studies to be a pastor, the word "mentor" was never used. One had an academic advisor, but the role of that person was limited to providing counsel regarding course selection with a little bit of career advice thrown in for good measure. Going on to seminary studies, I had a faculty member whose title was also academic advisor. In addition to weekly advisee group gatherings, the advisor would occasionally have a personal conversation with individual students, but almost everything was done as a group, including social events. Few really personal conversations took place between the faculty advisor and the student.

Now, fifty years later, having served as a pastor for eight years and then as an administrator and faculty member of a seminary for over forty-five years before recently retiring, I have seen a seismic change in the whole area of mentoring. Mentoring simply was not a part of ministerial vocabulary years ago, but it is now taken for granted that mentoring will be part of the educational experience of students preparing for various Christian vocations. And mentoring has merged into a discipling process along the way, not only providing a presence in helping to develop leadership skills, but also aiding mentees in their spiritual development.

This change is good. My generation would have been helped by mentoring. I would have been helped by having a mentor. By nature, I am rather reserved and independent, thinking and behaving in a way that signals "I would rather do it myself, thank you very much!" It was naïve (perhaps even unintentionally arrogant) on my part, but I think it reflected much of the way leadership was done in the past. So, I've never been inclined to seek out a mentor, which I think has made me less effective than if I had someone to whom I could have gone to with questions and concerns about myself and ministry matters.

When Scott came to Gordon-Conwell Theological Seminary to begin his MDiv studies, I was his academic advisor, which at that time included some of what we now might call mentoring. But it was mostly advising on academic matters and leading small group worship and discussions on a weekly basis in the office for the advisees as a group. Scott would frequently stop by my office just to visit and talk about ministry matters. A friendship began to form that went beyond the usual faculty-student relationship.

When he went on to Oxford University in England for his DPhil, my wife and I had the privilege of visiting him one summer. Then, when he returned home and pastored a church in Pennsylvania we kept in regular touch with each other and talked about a variety of ministry tasks along the way. I was involved in his becoming a faculty member at Gordon-Conwell. That was a happy

FOREWORD

day, indeed, for the seminary, and now three decades later he has held (until the time of this publication) a professorship of preaching named for his mentor, the late Haddon W. Robinson.

Scott has often referred to me as one of his mentors, but in all honesty I must say that it has been an unintentional mentoring on my part. We have had a strong friendship for many years, one that I treasure. We have enjoyed some traveling together to conferences and seminars, and with our wives, some lovely social times together as well. Although he is twenty years my junior, it's been a collegial relationship all along. Any mentoring on my part, again, has been unintentional, which is not to say that it has been uncaring, but the initiative for it has most often come from Scott. Having said that, however, I would also say there is not much about life and ministry we have not talked about—to our mutual benefit. Does mentoring, then, go two ways?

Although I might refer to my mentoring as unintentional, it is clear that Scott is an intentional mentor. This book is an illustration of that reality. From his arrival as a faculty member at Gordon-Conwell, he has intentionally come alongside students as a friend and wise counselor, helping them develop as competent pastors, teachers, and ministry leaders. He has such a reputation for being an excellent mentor that students now seek him out for mentoring.

This book contains the stories of "Scott's boys" as they are affectionately referred to, and they are competent leaders in their own right. Only heaven knows the contribution to the kingdom of God that these men (and Patricia) have made and are making. Thanks be to God for people like Scott who are drawn to serve as a mentor to others on their way to significant leadership positions in the worldwide communion of God's people.

Kenneth L. Swetland
Emeritus Professor of Ministry
Gordon-Conwell Theological Seminary
South Hamilton, Massachusetts
December 2017

Acknowledgments

A COUPLE OF YEARS ago Stephen Sebastian approached me about the idea of collaborating on a book project to honor Scott M. Gibson. I am grateful to Stephen for his thoughtfulness and creativity. We want to thank Kenneth L. Swetland for writing the foreword and all of Scott's boys who have made this project viable through generosity in sharing their resources, stories, and time. Some of the boys wanted to write a reflection for this volume, but for various reasons were unable to do so. They want to express their love and appreciation for Scott as well: Jacob Akers, Rob Berreth, Keith Campbell, Jim Cheshire, Jairus Hallums, Tom Haugen, Patrick Lowthian, Stephen Nyakairu, Brannin Pitre, Deryk Richenburg, Eric Russ, Michael Spurlock, Jim Teall, Andy Tisdale, and Young-Kee Yu.

We want to thank our editor, Matt Wimer, and the entire staff at Wipf and Stock Publishers for their gracious support of this project and for bringing it to fruition. Finally, we give thanks to God for Rhonda—Scott's wonderful wife and our spiritual mother—who is a woman of noble character, remarkable hospitality, timely grace, and extraordinary love, and who is often serving behind the scenes but really deserves all of the appreciation and credit in the world.

Introduction

MATTHEW D. KIM

SCOTT MILLER GIBSON WAS born in New Castle, Pennsylvania, on April 28, 1957, to Bob and Jean Gibson. Coming from a non-Christian lineage, Scott and his three siblings didn't experience the nurturing of being raised in a Christian home. He first heard the gospel at the age of fourteen at Harmony Baptist Church in New Castle. It was there that he experienced life-on-life discipleship firsthand, being mentored and discipled by the late Reverend Paul R. LeVan[1] and spiritually mature couples who would become his new church family and share the Christian life with him.

Proverbs 20:24 is one of Scott's life verses: "A person's steps are directed by the Lord. How then can anyone understand their own way?" A preacher might summarize it like this: "God directs our lives and we depend on him." It's a Scriptural morsel concerning the nature of biblical wisdom. It's how a wise person might maneuver through the peaks, plateaus, and pitfalls of life. It's a verse penned by divine and human authors that has guided Scott step-by-step to this point. It's his continuous reminder of God's faithfulness and grace that he has shown to Scott over the course of his life, even during the most challenging seasons.

Like the Proverb instructs, Scott's entire journey has been directed by the Lord. After finishing his undergraduate degree in

---

1. For additional information about Paul R. Levan, see https://alamosanews.com/article/rev-paul-r-levan-86.

INTRODUCTION

education at Pennsylvania State University, Scott received his call to pastoral ministry, which led him to Gordon-Conwell Theological Seminary to train for his Master of Divinity and prepare for a life in the pastorate. He later completed Master of Theology degrees at both Princeton Theological Seminary and the University of Toronto and finished his terminal degree: a Doctor of Philosophy at Regent's Park College at Oxford University in church history, writing on the life, ministry, and preaching of Adoniram Judson Gordon (1836–1895)—the influential American Baptist minister in Boston. And yet, with all of his education and erudition, Scott's passion has always been to use his gifts for the sake of the church in order to pastor, preach, teach, mentor, counsel, and disciple God's people. His commitment to advancing Christ's kingdom has also led him to pastor churches in New York, Pennsylvania, and Massachusetts.

Over the years, God has used Scott to serve his kingdom in ways that Scott could never have understood or envisioned for himself. Among many things, he has been a leader and entrepreneur in the field of homiletics. He and the late Keith Willhite pioneered the Evangelical Homiletics Society (EHS) in 1997. EHS's membership has seen robust growth over the last twenty years with nearly three hundred members. Recently, the EHS honored Scott by naming a scholarship after him, the Scott M. Gibson Emerging Scholars Grant, for promising young homileticians. Scott is recognized by his colleagues around North America and around the world as a champion for the field of homiletics. His numerous preaching initiatives launched through the Haddon W. Robinson Center for Preaching has made Gordon-Conwell Theological Seminary a choice destination for students interested in preaching. One of his passions and life's pursuits has been to foster and develop faithful, evangelical preachers, homileticians, and teachers of preaching.

Second, Scott is an outstanding teacher. Clear, engaging, humorous, accessible, creative, and pastoral, he instructs future pastors with excellence. He loves his students, and his students reciprocate this love. He does not treat them like an impersonal identification number in a wooden school directory. Rather, he

Introduction

learns all of their names and cares for them by asking them questions about who they are, where they have come from, and what they aspire to be in the future. He has been invited to teach courses and give numerous lectureships at Bible colleges and seminaries, providing additional commentary about the quality of his teaching abilities.

Third, he is a prolific scholar. His list of publications is impressive. He has written or edited fifteen books, authored over 150 articles, sermons, and reviews, with other writing projects on the horizon. He has served with excellence as the general editor of *The Journal of the Evangelical Homiletics Society* for nearly twenty years. His scholarship is wide-ranging and speaks into various disciplines such as church history, theology, ministry, worship, missions, exegesis, hermeneutics, denominations, discipleship, preaching, and more.

Fourth, in honor of Scott's accomplishments, he has received a call (as of 1 July 2018) to Baylor University, George W. Truett Theological Seminary, to be the holder of the David E. Garland Chair of Preaching and the Director of the PhD program in Preaching. This chair underscores his lifetime of dedicated and distinguished service in ministry, teaching, and scholarship.

However, more valuable than all of these accomplishments and abilities, as impressive as they are, Scott would say are his treasures—his disciples—his children in the faith. Scott wedded his beloved Rhonda Aiken, who is like-minded in her commitment to mentoring and discipleship. Since their wedding day on December 15, 2000, the Gibsons have shown extraordinary hospitality to countless people in their home, and over the years together they have mentored nearly fifty students at Gordon-Conwell Theological Seminary—on a weekly basis—whom they affectionately refer to as "the boys," their spouses, families, and even others beyond the seminary campus.

This book is a collection of short reflections on mentoring and discipleship in honor of Scott M. Gibson. It speaks about mentoring and what a true and lasting discipling relationship can aspire to be. Scott often says: "The missing ingredient in the church

INTRODUCTION

today is discipleship." He's right. You probably feel this spiritual void in your congregation, too. He has taken the mantle of discipleship seriously, and his life has modeled this commitment with great efficacy.

The foreword is written by Kenneth L. Swetland, Scott's longtime mentor, who has modeled and enjoyed a Paul and Timothy-like relationship with him for decades. A number of Scott's disciples or "boys" have reflected on one of the following eight topics: 1) character, 2) hospitality, 3) marriage and family, 4) mentoring and discipleship, 5) pastoral ministry, 6) preaching, 7) teaching and academics, and 8) wisdom. These topics are a snapshot of the ways in which Scott has poured into our lives. Stephen Sebastian—one of the boys—who receives the credit for the genesis of this book, has written the afterword. To honor Scott, the boys want to share his legacy and influence both with him and with you—the readers of this book. Moreover, our hope is that the contents here will cast a vision for all believers for what mentoring and discipleship can look like in the local church, in Bible colleges and seminaries, and in Christian friendships.

Greg Ogden defines discipleship as "an intentional relationship in which we walk alongside other disciples in order to encourage, equip and challenge one another in love to grow toward maturity in Christ. This includes equipping the disciple to teach others as well."[2] As you read this book, Scott's intentional lifestyle of discipleship will fly off the pages. Discipleship, for Scott, is not about programs. It's not about reading a book or a study guide on discipleship. It's not about checking off boxes on a mandatory list of do's and don'ts. But it is about spending time (a lifetime) with people "encouraging, equipping, and challenging" them and seeing how the Bible intersects with their lives in every single way so that they may look more and more like Jesus Christ (Col 1:28[3]).

Sometimes, discipleship is as cheery and delightful as eating a vanilla buttercream cupcake with a mentor you love. At other

---

2. Ogden, *Discipleship Essentials*, 17.

3. Unless otherwise indicated, the standard Scripture translation used in this volume is the NIV.

Introduction

times, discipleship is messy, awkward, and even painful, because it deals with correcting our sinful appetites and our "proneness to wander." The title of this book reflects Scott's philosophy of discipleship: "No program but time, no book but the Bible." He has invested countless hours of time, his talents, and his treasures in each of his boys and has demonstrated how the Bible directs us in every part of our lives. Scott has gone the extra mile of loving us well: by calling us, clothing us, correcting us, crying with us, emailing us, encouraging us, feeding us, housing us, hugging us, laughing with us, pastoring us, planning with us, praying for us, preaching for us, rebuking us, sharing hobbies with us, texting us, training us, visiting us, writing us, and altogether sharing his life with us in many other forms that cannot be calculated or recompensed. In sum, he has either been the father figure we never had or the father figure we have always prayed for.

We hope that, as you read this book, you will be inspired by Scott M. Gibson's example to be selfless and intentional about mentoring and discipling others. Many of Scott's boys have also gone on to mentor others and to make disciples in their places of influence. We long to see a multiplying effect of true mentorship and discipleship rippling across congregations in North America and around the globe. Scott has spent his life prioritizing discipleship because he wants to look more and more like his Lord and Savior Jesus Christ, and he wants the same for others. Christians are disciples—maturing learners—who learn and receive their direction from Jesus Christ—the greatest Mentor of all.

Part One

Character

GLEN MASSEY

Cracks in My Character

Glen is associate pastor of discipleship and spiritual
formation at Southport Presbyterian Church in
Indianapolis, Indiana.

WE ALL HAVE CRACKS in our character, but be encouraged—Jesus shines through our weaknesses and imperfections. The calling to vocational ministry is a high calling. Whether pastoring a local church or training seminarians, character matters. In Dr. Scott Gibson's introductory preaching class, the first topic discussed is the character of the preacher. Before students learn the first thing about writing or delivering a sermon, it is stressed that the minister must be a person of integrity.

Character development is vital. A failure to make progress in our own spiritual formation has potential to seriously compromise our ability to help others. New Testament writers such as Paul and Peter even warn that it is possible for a minister of the gospel to become disqualified on account of poor character.[1] D. Martyn Lloyd-Jones says, "A man who has great problems himself and is in a state of perplexity is clearly not one who is fitted to be a preacher."[2]

---

1. See 1 Cor 9:24–27 and 2 Pet 1:5–8.
2. Lloyd-Jones, *Preaching and Preachers*, 121–22.

PART ONE: CHARACTER

And yet no one is perfect. We all have cracks in our character, but our cracks have capacity to make us more effective in helping others—so long as they do not turn into craters. Cracks become craters when we refuse to acknowledge and work on our character defects. When ignored, our flaws and shortcomings can grow into serious sins that disqualify us from vocational ministry.

Jimmy Dodd, leader of an organization called *PastorServe*, says every pastor has a maturity gap. Every vocational minister has a space between the persona others see on the platform and the reality of where the pastor actually is in his or her spiritual formation. "Let's face it," he says, "in the life of nearly every pastor, gifting exceeds maturity. And the gap . . . is fertile ground for hiding, secrets, abuse, and a series of dangerous sinful behaviors."[3] He says it is vital that we seek to make the space that exists between our maturity and our visible ministry as narrow as possible.

One way to grow in our character and minimize our maturity gap is to allow a mentor to help us to grow in our areas of weakness. Sadly, according to Dodd's research, four out of five pastors do not have this kind of person in their lives.[4]

Dr. Gibson has taken his role as a mentor very seriously in the lives of dozens of seminarians he has mentored over several decades. I first approached Scott in 1997 when I arrived at Gordon-Conwell and asked if we could spend some time together outside of the classroom. I had no idea how seriously he took mentoring. He asked me questions on a weekly basis about my marriage, soul, character development, relationship with God, and plans for the future. I eventually learned that our relationship would not end upon graduation—he was going to walk with me for life!

More than ten years after I graduated seminary, Dr. Gibson came to visit me. We spent time together, caught up on a number of topics, and then he asked me a pointed question: "What is it that you don't want to tell me?" The speed of my answer should have been a clue. "Nothing. There is nothing I don't want to tell you."

---

3. Dodd, *Survive or Thrive*, 59.
4. Dodd, *Survive or Thrive*, 246.

The truth is there was something I did not want to discuss. This was my opportunity to ask for help, but I refused. On one hand, I knew I was in over my head but on the other hand, I thought I could manage on my own. I fell into the trap that I warn others not to fall into. I thought I could work on my issues without any assistance from others—just me and Jesus—even though James 5:16 clearly says we are to confess our sins to one another so that we may be healed. Had I shared honestly with Scott that day, I would have saved myself additional troubles later on. Thankfully, I did eventually have the courage to open up to others before I made an even bigger mess of things.

It is often difficult to share our weaknesses with people in our congregations. For this reason, a mentor outside of the church or organization where we serve is likely preferred. A church member once told me, "We want to hold you up as a shining example of what could be!" This man wanted a pastor who had it all together—no visible or invisible flaws. When he said this, I felt an unbelievable amount of pressure. It is not easy to be "a shining example of what could be"; at least, not until we realize that the shining example is not our own moral perfection, but the light of the gospel shining through our imperfections.

Paul says in 2 Corinthians 4:7, "But we have this treasure in jars of clay, to show that the surpassing power belongs to God and not to us."[5] Every pastor and seminary professor is ultimately a cracked pot; thankfully, Jesus shines through the cracks in our character. One scholar says, "The beauty of containers made of earth is that their very weakness and baseness focus attention on God's extraordinary 'power.'"[6] The goal of ministry is not for others to see how great we are, but to see how awesome God is. Our human frailties and weaknesses keep the focus off of us and properly directed toward God.

Know that Jesus' "grace is sufficient for you."[7] As we share honestly with others and allow them to know us on a deeper level,

---

5. 2 Cor 4:7 (ESV).
6. Guthrie, *2 Corinthians*, 254.
7. 2 Cor 12:9.

we open the way for the gospel to shine through. So, you are in ministry and you do not have it all together? You are in good company. Find a mentor and work together on your character defects. Do not wait for others to approach you; take the initiative, and ask an older man or woman that you respect to walk with you and speak truth into your life.

Ken Shigematsu

Contagious Character

Ken is senior pastor of Tenth Church in Vancouver, British Columbia, and the author of *God in My Everything*.

Scientists have discovered that we human beings tend to imitate one another. In fact, our brains have specialized cells called mirror neurons that cause us to mimic what other people are doing. For example, if you are at a party and talking with someone, and the person grabs some chips from a bowl—even if you're not particularly hungry—you may find yourself unconsciously mirroring their behavior and reaching for the chips. If your conversation partner crosses their arms, moments later you may unconsciously cross your arms, too. These mirror neurons also help us to share the feelings of others. When someone walks into the office in a sour mood, you may feel worse yourself. Alternately, if you walk into a room where someone is laughing—even if you don't know what's so funny—you will most likely feel a smile cross your face. Television sitcoms use laugh tracks because they know that if you hear other people laughing (even a recording), you'll be more likely to laugh yourself.[1]

According to the philosopher René Girard, not only do we imitate other people's physical actions and emotions, we

---

1. McGonigal, *Willpower Instinct*, 188.

unconsciously mimic their desires.² Desires are contagious. Our relationships influence us, and we come to want what the people around us want. But unlike contracting a cold or flu virus, which can happen when we're among strangers or even the cashier we know at the supermarket, the transmission of desires and values isn't indiscriminate. Our relationship to someone determines how much we will be infected, or influenced, by them. The more we respect them, the more open we are to their influence, and the more infectious they will be.³

Scott Gibson is someone I deeply respect, and I've grown very close to him. His passion to live a Christ-centered life has been profoundly contagious, and he has had a deep influence on my life.

Time Together

I first met Scott when we both lived in a dorm called C-Level, which in the mid-nineties was located in the basement level of the Kerr Building at Gordon-Conwell's South Hamilton campus. We only exchanged a few sentences in the hallway, but I still remember being impressed by his warmth and genuine interest in me. Scott was pursuing doctoral research on A. J. Gordon at the time, and he had just started to teach preaching on an interim basis at the school. During my second and third years at seminary, Scott lived in an apartment called Graham Hall, one of the residences on campus. Each week he hosted me for a dinner that he cooked. We would talk about my studies and my life as a student, but he also asked questions such as:

> How is your relationship with God?
>
> What are some of your greatest challenges?
>
> Where are you being tempted?

---

2. Girard, *Deceit, Desire, and the Novel*, 12.
3. McGonigal, *Willpower Instinct*, 194–95.

I wasn't familiar with the term at the time, but Scott was offering what I now know as "spiritual direction." Our conversations helped me discern God's voice in my life.

Unconditional Love

Scott was also the face of God's unconditional love for me. One summer as a single student, I had a selfish, irresponsible romantic fling. Scott was one of the first people I disclosed this to. He wept, expressed his deep love for me, but also charged me to set needed boundaries. In retrospect, my failure and his loving, wise, courageous guidance helped me set the right foundation for what has become more than twenty years of subsequent pastoral ministry and leadership. As we know, skills are important for ministry, but character is even more important. Scott was not my preaching professor at seminary, but he served a much more important role in my life: he was my "character professor."

We continue to connect from time to time by phone and occasionally in person. He is one of the few people in my life who continues to ask me tough, penetrating questions—always motivated by love.

Taking Risks On Me

During my final year at Gordon-Conwell, Scott was organizing a preaching conference. The opening keynote speaker, a nationally respected expositor of the Scriptures, had to pull out of the conference a day or two before it was slated to begin. Scott tapped me on the shoulder and asked me if I could step in and deliver the opening keynote sermon. I declined, feeling like I didn't have the chops to be speaking to such an august gathering. However, I always remembered his confidence in me—even when I didn't share it.

Years later, Scott again invited me to speak, this time at Gordon-Conwell's inaugural national preaching conference. As he, Haddon Robinson, and I were walking up the hill toward what is now called

Kaiser Chapel to attend the opening session, I was silently rehearsing some of the lines for my sermon. Robinson put his arm around me and said, "Whatever you do—don't embarrass us!"

Given my limited preaching experience and my mediocre performance when I was a student in his preaching class, Robinson's hesitation was warranted. But I appreciated Scott's belief in me and his willingness to take a risk on me. He pushed me to reach further and helped me to grow in character and confidence as a human being and as a preacher.

Prayer

I deeply appreciate Scott's prayers for me. As I stand up to preach each Sunday, I know he has prayed for me (he prays for his "boys" on Sundays). Our work of proclaiming the gospel of Jesus Christ is profoundly spiritual. When we are engaged in it, we are battling against unseen forces in the spiritual realm (Eph 6:10–20). Therefore, I am deeply grateful for Scott's (and other people's) prayers. Through his ongoing faithful intercession, he has been a long-time partner in ministry.

I am profoundly grateful to God for the ways he has used Scott Gibson to shape my character by his generous offering of time, unconditional love, risks he has taken on me, and his prayers.

I have had many teachers, but few fathers. Scott has been a father to me in Christ.

Part Two

Hospitality

John Meinen

The Strange Power of Stranger-Love

John is a Reformed University Fellowship campus minister at the University of Vermont.

THERE IS A DIFFERENCE between knowing honey is sweet because you read so in a book versus knowing honey is sweet because you've tasted a spoonful. Likewise, there is a difference between knowing God is good and gracious because you've read so in a book versus knowing God is good and gracious because you've tasted and seen that he is. That difference shows up in hospitality.

What exactly is hospitality? Hospitality is often confused with entertaining—think immaculate living spaces, carefully folded napkins, glistening silverware. When we entertain, the goal (stated or not) is to impress others: "Look at me." Hospitality is very different. Hospitality is not about making an impression, but rather about extending an invitation, especially to someone who hasn't received one before. It's not about showing off, but rather it's about showing kindness. It is sacrificial, other-oriented love.

The Greek word for hospitality (*philoxenos*) is actually two words (*philo*, "love") and (*xenos*, "stranger") wedded together. Quite literally, to be hospitable means to love the stranger. Inviting friends over to dinner is certainly a nice thing to do, but it's not quite "hospitality." We are hospitable when we invite strangers into our home and initiate friendship with them. We are

PART TWO: HOSPITALITY

hospitable when we make outsiders, insiders. We are hospitable when we make the foreign feel familiar—better yet, like family. That is true hospitality.

Hospitality is certainly one of the main, overarching themes of the entire Bible. In the beginning, God made a home for us to dwell in with him. Nevertheless, we turned our backs on him. We ignored his voice and rebelled against his commands. Tragically, yet predictably, our sins have made a separation between God and humankind.[1] We have become estranged.[2] But God does not leave us as strangers. On the contrary, he pursues the whole of humanity with the goal of turning outsiders to insiders once again. This divine drama culminates in the sending of God's very own Son into the world to seek and save the lost. Jesus preaches about God's in-breaking kingdom, and eats and drinks with sinners; he invites us to sup with him, and washes our feet so we can eat what he has spread out before us. He is, in a word, hospitable.

Hospitality is transformative. "Few acts are more expressive of companionship than the shared meal.... Someone with whom we share food is likely to be our friend, or well on the way to becoming one."[3] When Christ (and by extension, when a Christian) sits down with "the other" and breaks bread with them; when he and we invite "the other" into our homes and treat them as family; sinners don't just hear about the grace of God. They experience it. They experience the stranger-love of God. And this changes them. It changes us. We come to know with head and heart that God loves us and that he wants to be with us. And this experiential, head-heart knowledge has the power to turn enemies of God into God's friends and transform seekers and skeptics of Christ into Christ's followers.

Consider this story told at the beginning of John's Gospel: In John 1, we find John the Baptist standing next to two of his own disciples: a man named Andrew and (for the sake of storytelling) another man named Gary. When Jesus walks by, John

1. Isa 59:2.
2. See Eph 2:12.
3. Steel, *Hungry City*, 212.

says to Andrew and Gary, "Behold! Look! The Lamb of God!" Hearing this, Andrew and Gary begin to follow behind Jesus. At this point, Andrew and Gary are still disciples of John and not disciples of Jesus. They are what many in the church would call "seekers." They've heard or read some things about Jesus, but they aren't sure if Jesus is legit. So what do they do? They study Jesus from a distance. Jesus permits this for a while. Eventually, inevitably, Jesus turns around and asks them: "What are you seeking?" Andrew and Gary's answer to Jesus' question implies that in order for them to come to a right knowledge about Jesus—"Is he for real or not?"—they need to spend time with him. They don't need to hear what others have to say about him—they need to hear from Jesus, the Word of God himself. Jesus answers their query with an invitation. "Come," he says, "and you will see." He shows them hospitality. Two outsiders become two insiders. Those who are unfamiliar with Jesus become familiar—they are treated like family. And this experience changes Andrew. The first thing he does is seek out his brother, Simon Peter, and says to him: "We have found the Messiah." "How can you be so sure?" we can imagine Simon saying back to his brother. "Come and you will see."

At the beginning of this story, Andrew was an estranged one, unfamiliar to Jesus. In the middle of this story, two outsiders are treated like insiders. At the end of this story, one recipient of Christ's hospitality extends the same hospitality to another estranged one; one outsider who was invited into a relationship starts inviting other outsiders as well. And, in the end, another life (Simon's) is transformed.

When I went to Gordon-Conwell Theological Seminary (GCTS) in 2008, I did so as a brand-new believer in Jesus. I went to seminary because I wanted to do exegesis and learn more about the goodness and grace of God. I sought head knowledge. But I got more than I bargained for. Week in and week out, I was invited to dinner at the Gibson's home. I entered their house a stranger—I left feeling like family. The Gibson's weekly dinners reinforced what I was learning in the classroom: that God loves me and wants to be with me. GCTS taught me about the goodness and grace of God, and at the Gibson house I got to experience these godly characteristics. Thanks to their stranger-love, I got to "taste and see that God is good" again and again. For that, I am forever grateful.

Tim A. Norton

Little Moments (Without Eggplant)

Tim is associate pastor of missions at First Presbyterian Church, an ECO Presbyterian congregation, in Winston-Salem, North Carolina.

I HATE EGGPLANT.
    I'm not proud of it, but it's true. My body is ruthlessly discerning in its efforts to find and reject any eggplant slices, chunks, or particles that may be present in a given dish. Imagine my dread when I sat down at the kitchen table for my first dinner at Scott Gibson's house, and he served a pasta dish filled with eggplant. Embarrassed doesn't begin to capture my reaction. I dodged and picked my way around those purple pieces of torture while rehearsing my internal shame narrative. "What is wrong with me?" I thought. "They're going to hate me. Why can't I eat like a normal person? It *looks* good. Why can't pretty food *taste* good? What a worthless fool I am." As expected, it wasn't long before I was exposed as a picky eater and a direct threat to the culinary standards which the Gibson family was accustomed to enjoying. I seriously considered rejecting the next dinner invitation because I was so stifled with shame. Looking back, it's clear that I needed a big moment of Christ's redemption.
    Shortly after the eggplant incident, something remarkable happened. I accepted one more invitation to the Gibson's for dinner

and discovered a blank index card on my placemat. With the index card came a request: write down meals which you confidently will eat. With Scott's encouragement, I responded with a few ideas that quickly became the served meals over the next four or five weeks: hot dogs, baked chicken, and other hopelessly bland food.

As I reflect on the impact of this little moment of hospitality, I'm reminded of Paul's relationship with the Galatians. Galatians 4:12 says, "I plead with you, brothers and sisters, become like me, for I became like you." In the context of the letter, Paul writes to the churches in Galatia who are tempted to trust Old Covenant law-keeping as a way of completing the work of Christ. In response, Paul essentially says, in my own words, "I used to live under the Law, but I became like you Gentiles who didn't even know the Law. I gave up my cultural comforts and immersed myself in your languages, customs, and practices so that I could show you gospel freedom and preach Christ with credibility. Since I've become like you in these ways, now become like me and receive this free grace."

While the passage is rich in theological and pastoral implications, Christians have rightly and particularly noticed in this verse a model for ministry. Today, faithful men and women are sacrificing their food, language, and geographic context in order to immerse themselves in the everyday lives of others so that Christ can be preached with credibility and specificity. On a much smaller but just as impactful scale, Scott gave up an evening every week which he could've shared one-on-one with his wife, Rhonda. He then forfeited his mealtime practices when he could've demanded that I adjust to their standards.

In the moment, the index card was trivial; however, gestures like this continued over time and formed a bridge of trust between us. I slowly began to open dark places of my soul because I knew a mentor who was willing to engage my dietary baggage without shaming me was also someone who just might be willing to enter my brokenness in a similar fashion. Indeed, those big moments of redemption eventually came. Scott preached Christ into my shame, challenged me to repent from my habitual sin, and counseled me through life's struggles. The Lord was faithful to work big moments of redemption through my relationship with Scott. But the big moments would never have come without the little moments of trading eggplants for hotdogs. This, as I've come to learn, is the nature of mentoring, in general, and hospitality, in particular. It occurs mostly in mundane situations. Indeed, hospitality in the little moments makes room for grace in the big moments.

On the surface, the index card was a small moment of hospitality and a seemingly unimportant decision. Scott had invited me into a mentoring relationship, which involved a weekly dinner at his home. The Gibsons wanted me to actually eat what they served, and the card insured this would occur. I doubt they thought much about the relational and spiritual impact of that 3 x 5 token of grace. Yet, for me, this small act of kindness paved the way for the gospel. In today's world, hospitality may often strike us as trite or even gender-specific. How far from the truth! In the hands of our Lord, ordinary hospitality is a powerful demonstration of the sacrificial commitment of Christ. A simple series of dinners and a silly index card forever changed my life because hospitality in the little moments makes room for grace in the big moments.

I would not be the man that I am today without Scott. Through his faithful presence, I became more grounded in my relationship with Christ and secure in my identity as a pastor and as a believer. He changed my life and continues to disciple me as a spiritual father. (Yes, he's even pushed me to enjoy a wide variety of foods!) Significantly, none of this would've happened if he didn't first demonstrate his commitment to me with sacrificial hospitality in the seemingly insignificant matter of meal planning.

Are we willing to do that? In a world that often celebrates impersonal discipleship programs with shortcuts to the big moments, are we willing to prioritize the lackluster discipline of faithful presence and ordinary hospitality? Are we willing to pursue the mundane moments as the building blocks of Christ's kingdom? After all, it was through a failed battle with eggplant around Scott Gibson's kitchen table that Christ rescued me from sin and shame. It was through the little moments of Scott's hospitality that Christ made room for grace in his big moments of redemption.

Larry Torres

Hospitality to Admire

Larry is an MDiv student at Gordon-Conwell Theological Seminary and a pastoral intern at Grace Community Church in Marblehead, Massachusetts.

GENERALLY SPEAKING, EASTERN CULTURES are more hospitable than Western cultures. People in the East tend to open up their homes primarily out of a sense of duty, and guests are usually shown respect. Not honoring and welcoming a guest would be shameful in many Eastern cultures. Here, in the United States, we tend to be more concerned with our privacy and personal space. We are often individualistic, which means hospitality does not come as naturally for us. The home is a sacred place where one retreats to and finds peace, and being willing to share that space with others is what hospitality is all about. Hospitality is a key component in discipleship. Yes, hospitality means welcoming and receiving guests and visitors, but it also means sharing your life and welcoming others into it. This is what Jesus did:

> The next day John was there again with two of his disciples. When he saw Jesus passing by, he said, "Look, the Lamb of God!"

> When the two disciples heard him say this, they followed Jesus. Turning around, Jesus saw them following and asked, "What do you want?"
>
> They said, "Rabbi" (which means "Teacher"), "where are you staying?"
>
> "Come," he replied, "and you will see."
>
> So they went and saw where he was staying, and they spent that day with him. It was about four in the afternoon. (John 1:35–39)

We see that Jesus invited these two disciples to come and see. Jesus opened up and shared his life with these men. An important part of discipleship is inviting others to come and see. It means allowing others to see your life and how Jesus Christ has truly changed your life and the way you live. That way, the ones who are being discipled can be encouraged and challenged to live a life that reflects the truth of the gospel. Scripture is clear on the importance of hospitality, both in the Old and New Testaments.

Hospitality is where discipleship begins. Jesus said "come and you will see." Then Jesus went on to make twelve disciples who would go on and make more disciples. Someone who is being mentored should be invited into the life and home of the mentor so they can come and see, because this is what Jesus did. The mentee should be able to see how the life of the mentor has been affected by Jesus Christ, and this should encourage the mentee to do likewise and seek more of Jesus in every area of life. Scott has invited me into his life and has shown me what God has done in it.

As Scott has mentored me, he has invited me to come and see. Every week Scott has opened up his home to me. Every Monday evening, I share a meal with Scott and his wife, Rhonda. This has meant a lot to me, especially being a seminarian that does not have much. We enjoy dinner and dessert together, and afterwards Scott and I spend some time in his den sharing what is happening in our lives. We also spend time in the Scripture and praying for each other. This is a time I look forward to every week, and a time I have cherished since starting seminary.

Part Two: Hospitality

The fact that discipleship takes place in his home shows how much Scott's boys mean to him. Scott's relationship with all his boys means so much to him that his home is a place that he shares with them. His home is not just a place he opens up on special occasions. It is a place that he and Rhonda open up on a weekly basis to myself and other boys. His home is the primary place where mentoring and discipleship happen. This makes discipleship and mentoring less formal and more intimate. Scott says, "No program but time, no book but the Bible," and his home is part of his discipleship philosophy.

One of my fondest memories in their home was last year on Christmas day. At the end of the night, they gave me a bunch of presents from "Santa Claus." They watched as I opened my presents, and they treated me as if I was their son. I received many great gifts, including my first bow tie. It is a moment I will cherish, and it was a time where I felt at home in their home.

An adjective I would use to describe Scott and Rhonda is hospitable. The way their home is set up is inviting to other people. Their home has been organized in a way that they can be hospitable to others. In fact, when they host people, they have a little sign on their kitchen island that says "welcome," and then they insert the guest's name there. It is clear that being hospitable is important to them. Scott and Rhonda have set a great example for me, and I'm sure many other people who have been to their home. I hope that one day I can be as hospitable as they are: being willing to open up my home and share my life with others, and showing the love of Christ through hospitality as they do. Their hospitality is truly something to admire, and it has had a great effect on my life and on the lives of others.

Jeff White

There's No Place Like Home for Discipleship

Jeff is assistant pastor of leadership development at Las Tierras Community Church (PCA) in El Paso, Texas.

Sharing meals together in the pastor's home has long been part of the preparation of young Christian pastors and leaders wishing to enter vocational ministry. Whether it came from theological discussions at Martin Luther's dinner table like those recorded in *Table Talk*, or from seminarians sharing life together with Dietrich Bonhoeffer—as discussed in *Life Together*—life in close proximity is an important part of mentorship for the ministry. Leaders showing hospitality is an important part of the spiritual preparation of young Christians in ministry for a couple of basic reasons.

Hospitality demonstrates Christian character to those who are mentored

One of the great values of hospitality is that it enables people to see how their mentors live. Paul speaks of the importance of younger Christians seeing the lives and character of their spiritual elders. To a group of Christians who were enamored with celebrity preachers, Paul reiterated the value of the personal, familial mentorship they had with him. "For though you have countless guides in Christ, you do not have many fathers. For I became your father in Christ Jesus through the gospel. I urge you, then, be imitators of me" (1 Cor 4:15–16, ESV). And to his beloved Philippians, he exhorted, "Brothers, join in imitating me, and keep your eyes on those who walk according to the example you have in us" (Phil 3:17, ESV). Imitation is a significant part of discipleship.

Yet, how can a younger Christian imitate a more mature Christian if they don't see the everyday lives and homes of their mentors? Life's victories and struggles, joys and sorrows are often felt most deeply at home. Our true character is often evident at home. In order for those we mentor to grow in their character, they need to be invited into the places where they see their mentor's life in action. Hospitality is a vital ministry in which the character of a mentor is demonstrated and can be imitated by younger Christians.

As a young couple, my wife and I were invited to Scott and Rhonda's home for dinner every Thursday night. It was during those dinners in their home that we saw what it was like for a husband and wife to work together in ministry. Whether they were hosting my wife and me or large groups for holiday meals, they set an example of sacrificial service and teamwork done in such a way that all who entered their home felt welcome. They also demonstrated care for the whole flock of God's people. During holidays or special get-togethers, they always made sure to include anybody and everybody in a way that made each feel appreciated. It was through their hospitality that I saw Scott and Rhonda's regular sacrifice for others, teamwork in ministry, and care for all people.

Hospitality develops Christian character in those who are mentored

The home is a personal place. It is not a public space, like a coffee shop or school, in which strangers come and go. Many people may be visitors at a home, even some who the host does not know, but in such cases, the strangers quickly become acquainted and are invited into the familiarity of the home. The home is a personal and familiar place. It is an intimate space; and therefore, a natural environment in which trust, warmth, and openness is cultivated.

Younger Christians need to sense the freedom to be honest, reflect, repent, and share their dearest hopes and dreams in order to grow in Christian maturity. They need places that are hospitable for crying over the bad to laughing at the good without judgment; but with exhortation towards godliness. When pastors or mentors open up their home, they are opening their personal and intimate space to mentees. When an elder Christian serves a younger Christian in his or her home, they demonstrate care for the one they mentor. These things are necessary for a younger Christian to be able to reflect and to be honest with a mentor and therefore grow.

Frequently after dinner, Scott and I would watch baseball in the den. He always made sure I had dessert (mostly because I think he wanted dessert) or a snack. He always made sure I was cared for, and I knew that as we sat and watched baseball he was there to talk to and to listen to me. It was in that warm and inviting space that I felt like I could trust Scott to share the burdens on my heart. I could dream with him about my hopes and aspirations while asking for guidance. I could also share with him the struggles and difficulties I faced. Most of all, it was in this context where we could pray unhurriedly and meet with God together.

It is fine to meet at coffee shops or schools or church buildings, but these are the natural places for acquaintances, students, or parishioners. Yet, for discipleship to be effective, it must go deeper. It must go to the depths of sharing of our own selves with great affection. As Paul wrote, "So, being affectionately desirous of you, we were ready to share with you not only the gospel of God, but also our own selves, because you had become very dear to us" (1 Thess 2:6–8, ESV). The home is a natural place for such affection and sharing of our own selves to take place. Hospitality helps us get to this deeper level of discipleship.

Part Three

Marriage and Family

Earl Arnold

Family

Earl is a television actor, entrepreneur, lay minister, husband, and father of four.

"Come see a man who knew all about the things I did, who knows me inside and out.
Do you think this could be the Messiah?" And they went out to see for themselves.
—John 4:30 (MSG)

A man who has friends must himself be friendly,
But there is a friend that sticks closer than a brother.
—Prov 18:24 (NKJV)

WE GET TO MAKE a lot of choices in life, but there are some choices that were made for us, before we had the chance to say anything. Before we could think, reason, or speak, providence dropped us off at birth in a specific century, inside the borders of a country, encased in a one-of-a-kind body, and surrounded by a biological family that was not of our choosing. While time, location, and our physical frame may have their own benefits and liabilities, our nuclear families call for some serious reflection and understanding. After all, much of who we are or who we will become is tied to our family history; both for the good and for the bad.

PART THREE: MARRIAGE AND FAMILY

In John chapter 4, Jesus crosses paths with a Samaritan woman with some disreputable family history. She is at a local well drawing water when Jesus asks her for a drink. Quite a request, given that she's from a people group despised by the Jews. "How come you, a Jew, are asking me, a Samaritan woman, for a drink?"[1] This one question leads to an interaction with Jesus that exposes the woman's failures and fractured family life, invites her into Jesus' family, and explains to her how she can love and worship her heavenly Father.

I landed at Gordon-Conwell Theological Seminary in 1995 at the age of twenty-eight, trying to make sense of just about everything, including my own family history. I brought with me a bucketload of theological questions, but even more importantly, some personal issues through which I was working. I had grown up with some incredibly complex and painful family dynamics. On the surface, I had come to seminary for additional education and ministry training, but I was in need of more than knowledge and technique. I needed a friend's understanding and emotional release.

I met Scott Gibson at the theological well of seminary where we shared our drink to begin our friendship. He invited a few students to his office for a new student orientation coffee—offering hospitality and support. During our short interaction, I noticed Scott was sincerely interested in me as well as in my story. Much like Jesus with the Samaritan woman, Scott seemed to have time, in the midst of all the activity and hustle, to answer and ask a few questions that moved beyond small talk. His genuine curiosity caught my attention and made me feel welcomed and valued.

Jesus engages the Samaritan woman in more than small talk in verse 18. He points out that he knows her family's broken history. He also knows the truth about her and all things related to God the Father. After she explains that she has no husband, he says to her: "That's nicely put: 'I have no husband.' You've had five husbands, and the man you're living with now isn't even your husband."[2] Jesus pulls no punches here; making it clear that he knows her shameful past, he shows no condemnation. The woman's response in short is

1. John 4:9 (MSG).
2. John 4:17–18 (MSG).

this: You see me and know all. Can you tell me more about how I can know and worship God, since you're obviously a prophet that sees all things? In a life-defining moment for this woman, full disclosure and vulnerability with Jesus lead to deeper intimacy, more questions, and more life-giving answers. This grace-filled interaction with Jesus, for the first time in this woman's life, opens the door to faith, hope, and ultimately love.

Much like the Samaritan woman, my own family history contains secrets, betrayal, and shame—things only God has seen fully. The illness of addiction plagued my family for generations. Duplicity among family members was commonplace, and the wounds of sin and hypocrisy run deep. Due to my family's dysfunction, I have often looked for safe people whom I could trust. Researcher Brené Brown says: "Vulnerability is . . . the birthplace of connection and the path to the feeling of worthiness."[3] I have always looked for connection with people who might see me as Jesus does—worth being known despite all of the baggage. Scott Gibson is one of those people I have found along the way that has offered honest connection. Over dinners, sitting at the ice cream stand, and walking on the beach, Scott gave me the space to share my story, as well as my hopes, fears, and aspirations. He offered a listening ear, acceptance, understanding, and encouragement. He was never surprised by my mistakes and failures. And, in the process, because of his friendship, increased feelings of worthiness grew in me.

The Samaritan woman, after being exposed but not rejected, moves to the most important question of all: "How can I worship God?" Jesus responds:

> It's who you are and the way you live that count before God. Your worship must engage your spirit in the pursuit of truth. That's the kind of people the Father is out looking for: those who are simply and honestly themselves before him in their worship. God is sheer being itself—Spirit. Those who worship him must do it out of their very being, their spirits, their true selves, in adoration. (John 4:24, MSG)

---

3. Brown, "Power of Vulnerability," 12:40.

Part Three: Marriage and Family

Take your true self to God our Father and adore him. Is this not the spiritual process for the Samaritan woman? Is she not presenting her true self to God, incarnated in the person of Jesus, showing her authentic self in all its uniqueness and brokenness? And she excitedly adores Jesus when she exclaims to her friends: "Come see a man who knew all about the things I did, who knows me inside and out. Do you think this could be the Messiah?"[4] Her story inspires others in the village to meet Jesus. After spending two days with him, the villagers proclaim: "We're no longer taking this on your say-so. We've heard it for ourselves and know it for sure. He's the Savior of the world!"[5] Jesus is the savior of the world, and the savior to those who adoringly bow before him in response to his unconditional love.

It's no coincidence that Jesus is speaking in terms of family: "That's the kind of people the Father is looking for; those who are simply and honestly themselves before him in their worship."[6] God, our Father, is instituting a new family where a loving Father takes his children as they are, as he transforms each member. There is only one requirement: that you, in humility, present your whole self to God the Father as Jesus' grace covers your failures and heals you by his sacrificial love.

Providence without grace can feel like a curse. Our circumstances become traps, our bodies become tombs, and our family only becomes inherited dysfunction. But when grace intervenes, direction and purpose are discovered, broken desires are liberated, and families are healed. The means of grace, Jesus, is often working through everyday people who are available in everyday situations. It can happen over a drink, on the golf course, or at the supermarket. Grace can transform the simplest of conversations into fountains of life. And through these connections, people are welcomed and adopted into God's family—confirming what God had planned all along. The Apostle Paul put it this way: "Long before he laid down earth's foundations, he had us in mind, had

---

4. John 4:28–30 (MSG).
5. John 4:42 (MSG).
6. John 4:23 (MSG).

settled on us as the focus of his love, to be made whole and holy by his love. Long, long ago he decided to adopt us into his family through Jesus Christ."[7]

Long ago, he decided to adopt us into his family. Our choices may seem limited and our context dire, but God's choices save and liberate. He does as he chooses, extending grace to whom he will. His grace welcomes the broken-hearted, makes friends into brothers, heals families, and builds God's eternal, universal Church.

Ultimately God's grace will restore all things created. After his resurrection, Jesus proclaimed: "I am making everything new! Write this down, for these words are trustworthy and true."[8] Trustworthy words that are true. All the big decisions have been made. We can rest in God's merciful providence.

---

7. Eph 1:4–6 (MSG).
8. Rev 21:5.

Benjamin C. Crelin

Mentorship
Adoption into Family Life

Benjamin is an MDiv student at Gordon-Conwell Theological Seminary and a candidate for ministry.

Proverbs describes the importance of a father mentoring his child: "Train up a child in the way he should go, even when he is old he will not depart from it."[1] As a mentor, Scott Gibson is much like a father to all his boys. Therefore, it is appropriate that I have learned much about family and marriage from him. Let me share a few examples.

Admittedly, Scott and I have never read books on marriage and family together. However, Scott has taught me much through his relational approach to mentoring. First, Scott and Rhonda model one expression of a healthy, God-honoring marriage. They're teammates in everything! The moment I walk through their door they both welcome me inside. They almost always make dinner together, with each person sharing part of the responsibility for the salad or bread or meatballs or stuffed peppers. After dinner, I hear one suggesting to the other to take the leftovers for their lunch the next day, and then they intuitively divvy up the kitchen clean-up duties. One will wash and rinse the dishes, while

---

1. Prov 22:6 (NASB).

the other wipes down the counters and puts away the food. Their synergy and mutual affection is obvious. From start to finish, they demonstrate that a marriage is about teamwork and service to one another. They even show that service is joyful in partnership!

In addition to building up the individual couple, Scott has also shown me another purpose for marriage. A godly marriage will naturally bless others. In fact, serving and caring for each other is primarily how Scott and Rhonda bless others. Their marriage acts as a fueling station. They fill one another's tank so that they can launch off to look to others. I'm one case in point. Rhonda supports and cheers on Scott so that he is freed up and empowered to spend several evenings a week with his boys. They even host a dinner once a month in their home for all of Scott's students who are pursuing a ThM in preaching. In similar fashion, Scott cares for Rhonda. Recently, Scott accompanied Rhonda to Pennsylvania for an Alumni Council meeting at her alma mater, Grove City College. Though this was a trip only Rhonda needed to make, Scott went to support her. Through that meeting, Rhonda was able to contribute in such a way that benefited the college. In addition, on holidays, such as Easter and Thanksgiving, they invite family and friends to join them so that no one is alone. This past Thanksgiving, my fiancée, Hope Edwards, and I joined the Gibson's and Rhonda's parents for dinner, along with other friends. Scott and Rhonda had a full plate with work and travel commitments, and yet they slaved away all day to prepare a wonderful meal to give us a home away from home. The revolving door of their home continues to bless others.

In other ways, Scott more directly teaches me about marriage as I prepare for it myself. He prays for me and my fiancée, and regularly helps me discern how I might best care for Hope. One time readily comes to mind. I went to Scott to seek his counsel on a job offer. It was a tough decision. I had been offered a generous job at a new church. I had to weigh the pros and cons of how the job would affect both of us. Scott counseled me to demonstrate through this decision what my lifelong posture would be like towards Hope. Would I put my job and desires first, or would I consider Hope's needs and prioritize her and our relationship? In hindsight, I am so thankful for Scott's advice. Hope and I decided to stay at our current church, and our relationship has significantly grown because of that decision. Hope knows that I will always endeavor to lay my life down for her so that we may flourish together.

Likewise, Scott has mentored me on how to treat family. He impresses me with the love he returns them, often warmly hosting family members for long stays. Though the Gibsons have never borne children, they have many boys! One of my fondest memories with Scott is when he and Rhonda took me to the Boston aquarium. We drove into the city together and enjoyed an evening with the sea lions, starfish, and sharks. It was an enjoyable family evening out. How Scott invests in his adult children gives me a deep appreciation for and desire to do the same. After his boys fly the coup upon graduating seminary, he continues the relationships, albeit often from long distance: talking on the phone with them, hunting with them, comforting them during hard seasons, and even performing their ordination services or officiating their weddings. Scott does not just mentor his boys for a season, but he walks alongside them for life. His boys are his family, and he will correct them, celebrate with them, cry with them, and champion them as a father would do.

Mentoring someone is not a program of rules. It cannot be taught from a book. Mentorship is the overflow of relationship forged through time and through mutual love. Scott has formed me simply by adopting me into his life. I am thankful for Scott, who has trained me up in godly ways of marriage and family, so that when I am older, I will not depart from the way I should go.

Kyle Lincoln

No Replacement for Family Time

Kyle lives in Scotland with his wife, Elissa, and is a research student in homiletics at the University of Edinburgh.

While Scott Gibson's commitment to biblical preaching has no doubt been instructive to many contributors in this book, the example of his own marriage and his commitment to family have as well. In this reflection, I pull together a few lessons and reflect on two Scripture passages that came to life as I got to know Scott and his wife, Rhonda.

Both passages are found in 1 Corinthians. Paul writes to the Corinthian church: "For though you have countless guides in Christ, you do not have many fathers. For I became your father in Christ Jesus through the gospel."[1] Knowing that people need parents to grow up spiritually, Paul offers to fill that role in the Corinthian church. Towards a similar end, he offers to be put under the spotlight. He writes, "Be imitators of me, as I am of Christ."[2] Paul isn't perfect—he never claims to be perfect—but he is willing to fill a role and to be a role model, an example.

Scott was one of the first people I met when I started at Gordon-Conwell Theological Seminary. A former student of his

1. 1 Cor 4:15 (ESV).
2. 1 Cor 11:1 (ESV).

introduced us over email during orientation week. Then, a few hours after receiving the email, Scott and I met during "Dessert Night with a Faculty Member." I was part of a group of ten or so students assigned to the Gibson's home for a dessert meet-and-greet. After arranging to get coffee later that week, we began to pray about whether we felt called to enter into a mentor-mentee relationship. Scott described his theology of discipleship and told me that this mentoring relationship, should we choose it, was "for life."

What I didn't realize at the time when I agreed to be mentored was that Scott was willing to fill a role in my life. Exceeding my hopes for a mentor relationship during seminary, Scott invited me into his family and became like a dad to me. I think it's also worth saying that Scott didn't try to replace my family of origin, but actually encouraged me to be a better son to my mom and a better brother to my sisters.

In my growing-up years, I lacked an example of what a marriage should look like. I saw marriages in the movies and occasionally saw my friends' parents together, but my own parents separated when I was in the sixth grade and later divorced. I didn't see the day-to-day of preparing dinner, dealing with the stresses of work, getting involved at church and in the community, planning, budgeting, dreaming, comforting, forgiving, and more. These are occasions for childhood observation—whether the example is good, bad, or (most likely) a mix of both—that one can take for granted. When I left home to attend college, I had dreams about getting married and starting a family. I desired to be for my children what my own father hadn't been for me, but I underestimated the importance of having an example of marriage. It was only when I started dating that I came face-to-face with my own internal struggle. I was nervous to admit that I didn't know what I was doing. I barely even knew how to date, never mind what came next!

In many ways, Scott showed me what a loving marriage could look like by inviting me to "be an imitator" of his own marriage.

By inviting me for weekly dinner, I watched him and Rhonda interact affectionately as they prepared dinner and cleaned up. He opened his home to me on his best days, as well as on days where he felt tired and consumed by his work. Scott shared stories about their dating and engagement. As I was in a dating relationship at the time, I couldn't help but listen closely. Then, in one-on-one conversation after dinner in the television room, he and I talked and prayed together. We often talked about what marriage was like and, most valuably, I got to see it with my own eyes. Finally, in the summer before my last year in seminary, Scott officiated my own wedding and invited my wife, Elissa, into his family, too.

As I reflect on the lessons Scott taught me about marriage and family, it is the sheer quantity of time he is willing to give that comes to the fore. It appears there's always something to snatch up your time in academics. Last year, Scott was working simultaneously on four book projects. Yet, he opened his planner for me. There was time enough for Starbucks and Dunkin' Donuts runs; time for trips with our wives up to Portland, Maine, and down to Cape Cod, Massachusetts; time for summer picnic concerts and winter drives to view Christmas lights; time for a weekly invitation to dinner. The list above scratches the surface.

Giving of one's time is a form of generosity, and it is inherently sacrificial. It involves saying yes to one thing and no to another. At the heart of the idea "no program but time" is a commitment to the long view of discipleship. It involves time, and probably a lot of it. "Quality time" is considered to be one of the ways people give and receive love in relationships.[3] And it's worth saying—if my experience with Scott is at all instructive—quality time isn't enough. I remember a radio show where a dad suggests that it isn't quality time he's lacking with his children. It's quantity time.

Paul's approach to discipleship with the Corinthian church came to life when I met Scott. The Corinthians had plenty of "guides," or perhaps "teachers," but they lacked "fathers." The same was true for me; going through college and seminary, one can amass dozens

---

3. For context of the term "quality time," see Chapman, *5 Love Languages*, especially pages 19–26.

of teachers. Not many will extend themselves beyond their professional roles. Not many will offer to mentor you or ask for a lifetime commitment! Like Paul to the Corinthians, Scott is willing to fill a family role, to be a role model, and to give his time. I imagine and hope that it will have a ripple effect on many marriages and families.

Christopher H. Priestaf

Marriage, Family, and Mentors

Chris serves as senior pastor of Mount Bethel Lutheran Brethren Church in Mount Bethel, Pennsylvania.

SCOTT WAS THE FIRST mentor I ever had. I'm convinced it's why his voice remains among the loudest in my mind so many years later, even when he's not actually saying anything.

I remember him not saying anything once. At least I don't think he said anything. To be honest, the title of the book he handed me caught me so off guard that I don't remember whether he said anything or not. What I do remember was the yellowish cover and the bold title emblazed on it: *Intended for Pleasure: Sex Technique and Sexual Fulfillment in Christian Marriages*. What? How does someone even respond to that?

I went home with my new gift and was quickly joined in my humorous uncomfortableness by my wife of seven years, Suzanne. We both wondered, in a moment of true marital oneness, what motivated such a gift. We also agreed that the best place for it was on the shelf—the shelf located in the most remote, unused room of our rented apartment. Maybe someday it would make for a good story, we thought.

The book made four moves with us without one page ever being exposed to daylight. Then, almost five years later, the book got its break. I humbly admit the same was true for that part of my marriage relationship. I don't know if all of Scott's boys got the same book or not, but I do know that each pre-marital couple I now counsel gets the same gift, weirdness of the moment and all. Why? Because I discovered that, though the subject of the book might be uncomfortable, the contents of the book were absolutely necessary.

This little exchange, which is still comical to me, provides serious insight into mentors and mentoring. It taught me that mentors willingly delve into areas that are uncomfortable because mentors understand that some of the most uncomfortable areas are the most necessary areas. Let that idea settle in for a minute: mentors delve into some of the most uncomfortable areas because mentors understand that some of the most uncomfortable areas are the most necessary areas. It's easier for me to write that now than it was for me to see it then. At the time, I couldn't see that, though the book was uncomfortable, it was also necessary. Scott was willing to delve into the uncomfortable because he knew that the uncomfortable was also the necessary. No one ever went there with me. I'm so thankful that Scott was willing to be the first.

Perhaps this is a strange way to get where we are going. But, in my fourteen years of pastoring, twenty-one years of marriage, and fifteen years of parenting, I've come to realize that this lesson of combining the uncomfortable with the necessary is a primary stalwart of healthy relationships. The lesson reaches to the very foundation of mentoring, marriage, and family.

Here is what I mean. At their very core, mentoring, marriage, and family are about relationships, and quality relationships are fundamentally about vulnerability. But one of the greatest obstacles to vulnerability is discomfort. Think about it: We aren't fully vulnerable because we aren't fully comfortable sharing parts of our personhood, even with those we love. Most of us can remember being uncomfortable at the thought of sharing certain dreams and aspirations, certain fears and failures, certain frustrations and regrets, or about what brings pleasure and what doesn't. We can remember being uncomfortable sharing when we were wrong, or that pride ruled the day. In sum, we are so content hiding the uncomfortable that we ultimately lose our vulnerability. The real loser, though, is the relationship.

The same is true for families. I am the proud father of three girls. I am also a product of a home with only two boys. That makes most "girl talk" horribly uncomfortable for me. A girl's emotions operate in a whole different stratosphere than mine—and that's uncomfortable. Connections between what's happening with hormones and the mind baffle me—and that's uncomfortable. Boys, bodies, and besties occupy way more mental energy than I could've ever imagined—and that is uncomfortable. But here is what I know: in order for me to enter my girls' worlds, which is absolutely necessary, I must somehow deal with the uncomfortable. If I don't, I'll miss my girls altogether.

The reverse is also true. It is uncomfortable for my girls to talk about their feelings about boys with me. It is uncomfortable for them to talk about bodily changes with me. It is sometimes uncomfortable for them to talk about dreams, aspirations, and failures with me. But here is what we all have learned: the more willing we are to push through the uncomfortable, the more likely we are to experience the richness God intended for our relationships.

In mentoring, marriage, and family, the relationships are different. But the root is the same. The mentor who loves the one being mentored willingly delves into the uncomfortable because he knows the uncomfortable things are the necessary things. The husband who loves his wife willingly delves into the uncomfortable things because he knows that dealing with the uncomfortable things is necessary for experiencing the intimate things. The father who loves his child willingly delves into the uncomfortable things because he knows that dealing with the uncomfortable things is necessary to be able to deal with the heart things. The child who loves and trusts his parents intentionally pushes through the uncomfortable things to discover the wise things. Put your own name and circumstances wherever they fit. The lesson will still be the same: delving into the uncomfortable things is necessary for experiencing the richest of things.

Part Three: Marriage and Family

I first learned this lesson from Scott. I am so grateful I did, for I see it play out every day in my marriage with Suzanne and in my relationships with my girls: Kelsey, Liliana, and Addison. And all of us are the better for it.

Part Four

Mentoring and Discipleship

Chad Bryan

Three Principles of Mentorship

Chad serves as the director of student ministries at Grace Fellowship Church, a multi-site church near Albany, New York.

God brings the person; we extend the invitation

In the first week at seminary, an ice cream social took place on top of the seminary hill. I didn't want to go. I needed to study for a competency test the following morning. However, my wife and newfound friends urged me to at least attend the social gathering—so I did. Begrudgingly, I ate my ice cream and tried to keep conversations short. Almost out the door, a tall and lovely couple approached our group and began to make conversation. At that point, I felt I had paid my social dues and was ready to move on, so I didn't participate in the conversation. Near the end of the conversation, I discovered that this couple's last name was "Gibson"—alarms immediately sounded off in my head. "This is Scott Gibson!" I thought. "This is the man my undergraduate professor at Moody Bible Institute raved about and someone I needed to connect with!" But it was too late—my pathetic attitude was overwhelmingly evident, and any hope of redeeming the conversation had vanished.

As my wife drove us back down the seminary hill to our apartment, I was distraught. I had blown an opportunity to form a relationship that could drastically change my seminary experience. The next few days, I was discouraged and tried to shake off the regret.

However, several nights following the social gathering, I received a phone call.

"Hello, Chad. This is Dr. Gibson."

"Dr. Gibson?" I responded in shock.

"I have a small church where I am currently serving as the interim pastor. I was wondering if you'd like to join me and help by teaching Sunday School each week?"

I was astonished. "Dr. Gibson," I replied. "In all honesty, why are you choosing to ask *me* to do this? The other night I was so rude and dismissive."

Dr. Gibson concluded, "Well, I guess I like Moody guys."

In mentoring, it is God's job to bring us the person he'd like us to connect with, and it is our job to be obedient in extending an invitation. Do we brush away God's leading? Do we dismiss his prompting with the habitual phrase, "I'm just too busy?" Do we assume the person we would love to have mentor us is "too busy" to be asked? Or do we extend an invitation and see what God might have in store? Whether we are looking to play the role of mentor or mentee, we need to be willing to follow God's prompting—extend the invitation!

In mentorship, everything is "fair game"

When we invite someone into our lives as a source of mentorship, there is no area of our lives that should be off-limits. In mentorship, our lives should be an open book—any page, any chapter, anytime.

As I sat in Scott's office one afternoon, he asked me to take out my pen.

"Pen?" I responded. "I don't have a pen."

Scott's face looked irritably surprised. "What do you mean you don't have a pen? Of course you have one."

I frantically searched my book bag. "No, I don't have one."

Scott looked baffled.

"I can't believe you don't have a pen!"

I muttered and mumbled, uncertain as to how I should respond.

"You know what?" Scott stands up from his chair and walks back towards his desk. "I'm going to get you a pen."

Scott grabs a pen from his desk, firmly reaches the pen out to me and says, "Here. Now you have a pen. I don't *ever* want you walking around without a pen again."

As I later left Scott's office, I was thankful. I knew Scott saw my giftedness for preaching, but that afternoon Scott made it clear that he saw my potential for growing as a man of responsibility. When I accepted Scott's offer to mentor me, everything in my life was "fair game." When the purpose of mentorship is discipleship, mentorship cannot be limited to merely one area of a person's life. When we allow our lives to be an open book with the trusted people God has brought into our lives, we allow them to read not only our strengths but also our weaknesses; we allow these trusted people to speak into our blind spots.

Mentorship requires openness and presence

The best mentorship isn't a formal process. Effective mentorship is not centered on one hour per week and a scripted conversation. When we look at the life of Jesus, he and the disciples were in all kinds of situations—eating together, sitting by the fire, on a boat, with large crowds, at the synagogue, etc. Jesus was on a mission, and he brought the disciples along with him, using every moment as a discipleship opportunity.

The best mentorship is not a formulated process. Instead, the best mentorship, while still highly intentional, is often spontaneous conversations while living out daily life. For three years, I talked life with Scott—marriage, schoolwork, ministry, preaching, etc. Many of the most meaningful conversations were in the car. At least once per week, we had a forty-five-minute drive to the church where we were both serving. Scott didn't let the time pass in vain.

One of the greatest barriers in people taking part in mentorship is the fear of "I just don't have the time." You might not have the time for something additional, but you do have the time to make your current obligations more meaningful. Invite the special person God's placed on your heart to the grocery store with you. You have to make dinner tonight so ask the person to come help and eat with you! If exercise is part of your routine, find a gym that will allow that special person to join you!

The best mentorship does not always stick to the same calendar and script; instead, the best mentorship centers on openness and presence—no matter the circumstances you are in.

Bill Haley

How Would Jesus Mentor?

Bill is the executive director of Coracle and Associate Rector at The Falls Church Anglican.

THE ULTIMATE GOAL OF Christian discipleship is that we would become "Jesus with skin on." With Jesus himself living so fully in us, we indeed hope to become his hands, feet, and heart in the world. In that this is the goal of discipleship, the one who disciples must truly be Jesus to the one being discipled.

Scott Gibson was "Jesus with skin on" to me. He was the perfect mentor in a formative season of my life.

I was young, and Scott was actually young as well in 1991 when we began our mentoring relationship. We both lived in the basement dorm at Gordon-Conwell Theological Seminary, and both of us were students. Scott was busy finishing his DPhil. Even then, he began what would become a prime emphasis—perhaps the most influential one—of his ministry: taking a young man or two at a time and simply pouring into them with all he had to offer.

And Scott offered me much. Scott was willing to give as much as I was able to take, whether it was having weekly meals together, gathering for prayer, looking at Scripture, reading books together and discussing them, navigating crises, simply talking about life, talking (or arguing about) theology, even taking short trips around New England. One year when he asked what I wanted for my birthday, and I said "A tattoo." Scott said "Great!" He paid for it and may have gotten one for himself!

In that Scott was a perfect mentor for me, what he did in my case offers some key aspects of good mentoring.

- A good mentor prays. I have no doubt that Scott prayed constantly and faithfully for me throughout seminary, and that is surely one of the reasons I survived. His prayers have continued long afterward.

- A good mentor gives grace. In the wake of my mistakes, Scott was quick and constant in helping me work through them, as opposed to judging me for them. He balanced grace, wisdom, and firm guidance.

- A good mentor believes in the other. Scott had a deep belief in me, even when I struggled to find that confidence for myself. He was a constant encouragement in both word and deed.

- A good mentor is patient. Scott bore much of my youthful arrogance, and tolerated it while challenging it, without giving up on me because of it. He seemed to be able to see past rough edges to whatever goodness was on the inside.

- A good mentor facilitates opportunities. Scott seemed to be on the hunt for opportunities that were uniquely suited to me, and then helped make them possible. Experiences that Scott facilitated ended up being profoundly shaping in my life and ministry. Almost twenty-five years later, I can say truly that some experiences that Scott made possible were the most important parts of my development as a Christian and as a leader.

- A good mentor is available. Scott was readily available to me during seminary, even well after, and still. To have him do my wedding a good six years after our mentoring relationship in seminary was a great joy and testament to this.

- A good mentor loves. It was clear that Scott was motivated by love, generally and specifically. One would expect this from "Jesus with skin on."

While both a pastor and professor, Scott came to the conclusion early in his ministry that mentoring and discipleship mattered as much or more than these other forms of service. That he has been able to do all these things with excellence and with an impact is a testimony to his faithfulness, good stewardship, and God's grace, for which many can be grateful.

Scott has operated on the conviction that character formation matters as much (or more) than mere competencies, and that doing life together can be as important (or more) than what a student gets in the classroom.

I'm confident that one of the reasons I've continued to love and follow Jesus and lead others to him is because Scott Gibson was "Jesus with skin on" to me. In this way, Scott has not only been faithful to the vocation of one who disciples, but even to the vocation of a Christian.

When he enters glory, he may well hear Jesus say to him, "Well done, good and faithful mentor!"

Michael R. Mazzye

Three Pictures
One Image

Michael is the pastor of Renovation Church in
North Syracuse, New York.

The vast majority of pictures on our phones are meaningless. Each photograph reminds us of what we ate for dinner a couple weeks ago. It represents an impulsive hat purchase at the beach during a family vacation or a grocery list handwritten by our spouse to ensure we don't forget corn starch for baking blueberry pie. These images all too often take up space in our phones, yet lack meaning for our lives. However, the images on our walls and mantles tend to be quite different. They represent personal relationships. They beg for life-shaping stories to be told. Should someone visit my home or office, they might be drawn to three different pictures that on the surface seem disconnected in style, size, and color, but in reality weave together to convey a story of the impact one man can have on another through a mentoring relationship. These three pictures provide snapshots of a relationship with Dr. Scott Gibson, who follows through on his discipleship philosophy—"No program but time, no book but the Bible"—and profoundly shapes me as a man of God, a preacher of God's word, and a shepherd of Christ's people.

Above the red chair that furnishes my church office, there is a colorful hand-drawn cartoon that combines two seemingly disconnected worlds with the use of metaphor. While their newly purchased home was in a suburban context, Scott and Rhonda Gibson are dressed in the classic garb of the well-known picture, American Gothic. Flanked to each side of the Gibsons are two groups of four men whose heads grow atop golden-brown corn husks. While the photo is static, it accurately depicts a relational dynamic whereby Scott Gibson, with the support of his wife, Rhonda, tilled the ground of each of these men's hearts, including my own. Over meals in his home, we talked about life, marriage, fears, hopes, and dreams. He asked tough questions in the safety of a father-son relationship, giving me freedom to confess my deepest inner sins and struggles. He consistently held me accountable and patiently watched God enable me to defeat sin in areas of my life where I felt stuck. The image above the red chair is a reminder for me of how Scott's time-generous, biblically-grounded mentoring has shaped me as a man of God.

Eight feet to the right of the colorful cartoon there is a 4 x 6 photograph atop a bookshelf. Scott and I stand smiling in front of the altar in the chapel at Gordon-Conwell Theological Seminary, where I had just finished preaching a sermon as the recipient of an annual scholarship award in preaching. Thirty months prior, I awkwardly introduced myself to Dr. Gibson and asked him on the spot, "Will you teach me to preach?" As busy as he was, he agreed to invest in my development as a preacher far beyond the typical instruction any homiletics student would receive. For three years, Scott branded the "big idea" on my homiletical heart. His persistence in a faithful process of interpreting Scripture kept me focused on clarity in dogged pursuit of the "subject" and "complement" of a Bible passage. Scott was consumed with exegesis, authorial intent, and connecting this authoritative message with the congregation. Fifteen years into my preaching ministry, I start every Monday with those concerns in mind. This protects me from error as I submit soul and mind to the authoritative word of God and the original intention of the biblical author. Each moment I gaze upon this picture, I am motivated by both clarity and faithfulness. For without Scott's effective instruction in homiletics, I would not be the preacher I am today.

Set above my living room couch is a painting by a Christian Mali—a nineteenth-century German artist. The details are somewhat blurry, but the story is clear: the unnamed shepherd with staff in hand is leading, feeding, and protecting his sheep. This painting was Scott's gift to me upon ordination, and has often been a reminder to me of the unglamorous nature of biblical leadership in the Church. When I get discouraged, I study and stare at this painting. It reminds me that ministry isn't about me. It's about Christ and his people. It teaches me that Christ is leading, feeding, and protecting his flock through tough terrain and in the face of real spiritual threat. God also turns my eye to this painting when pride creeps in. When things are going well in ministry and people give me their approval, I find myself reminded that shepherding is serving. It's about serving Christ and his people. Scott exemplified this to me as I observed him shepherd others sacrificially. And, he shepherded me as he would a son. He showed me what pastoral ministry was and how to shepherd those under my care with time, Scripture, and meaningful connection. His example has shaped my understanding of leadership and inspired me to shepherd Christ's people faithfully.

A colorful cartoon, a small photograph, and a painting all put on display the kind of legacy Scott Gibson has had on my life through his intentional mentoring. And what brings them all together is the one image Scott had in mind for each one of his boys: the image of Christ. There are so many stories to be told and experiences to share that represent the power of mentoring. When those whom Scott has mentored gather, we share those stories. We use words to create pictures in our minds. But all of the boys who were mentored by Scott had one image in view: Jesus Christ. The truth and love we share together was always about conforming to the image of Christ. God used Scott's intentional investment of time and Scripture in us to make us more like Christ. Scott Gibson has left a mentoring legacy on my life that has profoundly shaped me as a man of God, a preacher of God's word, and a shepherd of Christ's people.

Derek Mondeau

What Scott Gibson Taught Me About Discipleship

Derek is pastor of discipleship and parish ministry at Third Church in Henrico, Virginia, where he lives with his wife, Sue, and their two boys, Fisher and Remi.

Scott Gibson taught me that I am loved wholly by the Godhead. One of Scott's frequent refrains during our times together went something like this, "The only God I know is Father, Son, and Spirit." It turns out the children's song "Jesus Loves Me" does not go far enough. The gospel is bigger than even that. Scott taught me that every act of God in Scripture is a triune act. This meant that it was not only Christ that loved and accepted me, but the Father and the Spirit as well. At Calvary, the Trinity itself was shattered for you and for me. In Christ, every part and parcel of God's self has received me as his own.

Scott also taught me that the life of a disciple is saturated in Scripture. Without fail, every week in his office, we would turn to Scripture to guide our discussion. This was no afterthought. We would wrestle with the themes in the text. What does this say about God? What does this say about us and the world God loves? And, of course, we always considered the big idea of each and every text.

Week after week, Scott showed me that ideas of Scripture must do their work in us if we are to follow Jesus.

I learned that, most of the time, discipleship is about showing up. I am amazed when I think back on Scott's consistency. We met every Thursday afternoon from 2:00 pm to 4:00 pm for two-and-a-half years. I cannot remember a time when Scott ever canceled on me. It is easy to think of our spiritual growth in singular, transformative moments. That can be true. But Scott pursued me with the same intentionality in the mundane as well as in the spectacular. His presence made a regular space for me to know and be known.

Very closely related to consistency is the importance of follow-through to disciple making. I graduated from Gordon-Conwell almost sixteen years ago. I have never lived closer than one thousand miles to Scott since graduation. Yet, Scott has been present. I have received a card from him for just about every major holiday and milestone of my life. On some occasions, I have received deep letters. The message was clear: I know you, I love you, and I am thinking of you.

Scott also modeled that discipleship is about submitting all of my life to Jesus. It was during these years of discipleship when I learned, to steal from Abraham Kuyper, that there is no part of Derek Mondeau over which Jesus Christ is not Lord. Therefore, no topic was off limits during our discipleship meetings. Family. Sex. Relationships. Politics. Daily times with Jesus. My fears and insecurities about failing as a husband, preacher, and student. All of me brought before all of him. Scott was the first person that taught me that all good work in theology results in Christ-like character. Anything else is suspect.

I also learned that sometimes the mark of true discipleship is measured in how we suffer. The risen Jesus said to doubting Thomas, "If you want to know who I am, you have to stick your hands into my wounds."[1] As Nicholas Wolterstorff says, "The wounds of Christ are his identity."[2] The One who defeated death forever kept the very wounds with which death marked him. And like Jesus,

---

1. John 20:27 (my paraphrase).
2. Wolterstorff, *Lament for a Son*, 92.

we need to bear our wounds to one another. They are a part of us. It was a sovereign mercy to me that, at the beginning of my life in ministry, Scott Gibson bore his wounds to me in our times together. As he struggled with chronic illness, like celiac disease, he did not hide the painful nights, the lethargy, the struggles, and the toll that it took on his body and soul. Scott also shared deeply of his loneliness and sporadic struggles as a single man into his forties. We prayed often for his holy desire to find a wife and to make a life together in the world—to experience dominion—with a daughter of Eve. And we wept. Often. This level of transparency had a marked impact on me. I saw it modeled by Scott Gibson first.

Scott Gibson taught me that discipleship is about celebrating well. Trust me when I say that Scott Gibson knows this. Nobody celebrates Scott Gibson better than Scott Gibson. I mean nobody. Scott could offer a master class in throwing parties for oneself. This might strike some people as odd. But I find it to be thoroughly biblical. Heaven rejoices over one sinner who repents. The new creation will have as its centerpiece the greatest party of all time—the wedding supper of the Lamb. That same God delights in me. "His banner over me is love."[3] I am someone worth celebrating. Scott Gibson taught me that.

Scott also taught me that, when you disciple someone, you love them through their successes and their failures. I am sad to say that it is true that I have failed Scott as a friend more than I have succeeded. I am horrible at long distance friendships. This weakness runs deep in me. I have sought growth in this area over the decades; but honestly, that maturation has been slow and painful work. In spite of all the years I have been inconsistent, all the times that I have not followed through, not sent a card, or made a call—Scott has never added to my shame. Through my successes and my failures, he has always told me what he tells everyone he has discipled: "You are still my boy."

This leads me to the last thing I want to highlight about what Scott Gibson has taught me about discipleship. Scott's discipleship, at its core, has been about the spiritual act of fathering. Scott has

3. Song 2:4 (NASB).

been a spiritual father to generations of young men. Scott Gibson taught me that you do not have to be married or have kids in order to be a spiritual papa. God has used Scott to re-father places long devastated in me. Through Scott's long-suffering love, good things began to take root once again in the soil of this young man's heart. I did not always believe this would be possible. And through his example, I slowly began to believe in new and deeper ways that I have a father in heaven who loves me with a forever love.

Everything Scott Gibson taught me about discipleship can be captured in these nine words written by the Apostle Paul in 1 Corinthian 11:1: "Be imitators of me, as I am of Christ" (ESV). This was Scott's secret to discipleship—love others like Jesus loves you. Scott is too humble to say this about himself. So I will say it for him, because it is true. We should all imitate Scott, because if we did, we would look more like Christ. And for this reason alone, I will always be proud to be known as one of Scott's boys.

Part Five

Pastoral Ministry

CASEY C. BARTON

Wholeness in the Pastoral Call

Casey is Ordained to Word and Sacrament in the Evangelical Covenant Church and is the senior pastor of Hilmar Covenant Church in Hilmar, California.

IN MY EXPERIENCE OF preaching and pastoral ministry over the past twenty years or so, I've realized that there are some pastors who are preachers at their core, and stand weekly to preach God's word because the fire in their hearts burns for proclamation. Yet, there are others who stand weekly to preach so that they may give themselves to hurting people and a world in need.

I have wondered at the rare individual who weaves together these two aspects of the pastoral call so seamlessly that you understand them not to be two things at all but only the wholeness of what pastoral ministry is supposed to be. And then, I wonder if it's not so much that the pastor has woven together two things so well, but really that the rest of us have somehow torn the one thing into two.

I look back at the years that I have known and been mentored by Scott Gibson, and there's no one I've known who has embodied this wholeness so well and then, simply by his embodiment of that wholeness, has taught wholeness to those he has mentored.

I stepped into seminary in the autumn of 2000 looking to learn how to preach. Or rather, let's be honest for a moment. I came in as most first-year students, looking to display my amazing preaching skills and have them be validated by an astonished faculty. I'm not sure what Scott saw in me—the sermons I preached never quite matched the high view I had of them—but I became his assistant, and he decided I needed mentoring. Really, Scott pastored me. By pastoring me, he taught me how to be a pastor. I wouldn't say I took to the lessons particularly well. Nearly twenty years later, I'm still working it out. But Scott did teach me what stands at the center of a holistic pastoral ministry. It is this simple and immeasurably deep philosophy/theology: no program but time, no book but the Bible.

No Book but The Bible

In all of my journeys through higher education, a commitment to Scripture has remained the core of my discipleship and preaching. This is because it has been impressed upon me: no book but the Bible.

It is fascinating how many different views of Scripture exist in the academic preaching literature of our day and in the pulpits across Christendom. For some, the sermon has its genesis here or there, or some other place altogether. For others, Scripture is incidental to the words spoken from the pulpit, and we are free to add or take away from the text depending on rhetorical, communal, or societal needs, as if it isn't God's word itself that our community or society needs. I've heard it in the philosophies of the academy, from preaching students as I've taught, and in pews where I've been the congregant.

Anyone who has ever taken a class from Scott, has read one of his books, or has engaged him in a serious conversation about preaching and pastoring, knows without exception that the Bible is the authority for the preacher's words. Sermons and ministry must be biblical. While issues of sermon form or methodology may evolve or change, this does not. It is a theology for preaching: there is no book but the Bible from which the pastor's words for the world derive. It is also a theology for pastoring: it is God's word that changes our lives. Those who would answer the pastoral call must be changed and formed by God's word as we encourage God's people to be formed and changed by it. There are no words that stand so central to the wholeness of our calling than God's.

It still strikes me as a gift that this simple and yet essential affirmation was impressed upon me by a mentor for whom God's word is life and breath: no book but the Bible. It is true of our preaching. It is true of our pastoring. It is true of our discipleship as followers of Christ.

No Program but Time

Time is the gift we're given from God, and it is a gift that we give to others. It is through time spent with others, and in prayer for others, that God grows the love between us and that, in turn, strengthens us on our journey through this world together. There is a discipline involved in giving your time to others. I happen to think that spending time with people, with the Holy Spirit beside us, waiting to see what God will do or say or sharpen in our interaction, committing to vulnerability with another, is a more difficult discipline than many others. That may be because I shake out on the more introverted side of the spectrum. Yet, for pastoral care, there really is no substitute for it. There is no gift like it.

Scott taught me this by being exceedingly generous with his time as I'd spend hours with him in his office as his assistant, or in his home as his guest and friend. When I struggled through more than a decade of severe chronic pain, and finally had brain surgery to remove a tumor, followed by a recovery as emotionally and spiritually taxing as the decade of pain itself, Scott sat in prayer for me. In dark moments of pastoral ministry that have thrown me into loneliness that I didn't imagine to be possible, Scott has been present, even if a few thousand miles away. And though I know that I have not been as faithful in giving him my time, he has extended grace upon grace, never giving up on one who does not reciprocate the gifts he's been given.

Isn't this the summary of discipleship? To give oneself to the life and care of another person? Our program is time.

Wholeness

This, it seems to me, is an image of a holistic pastoral ministry. I used to think I could hone my preaching, and the rest of ministry would take care of itself. As is so often the case, as the younger get older and realize the wisdom of others who have come before them, I have matured and grown into the calling that God has given me. And I've recognized that I can't simply be a preacher who lightly attends to those other pastoral things. There's a wholeness to this calling. A wholeness that has been exhibited to me in this simultaneously simple and sacred path: no program but time, no book but the Bible.

Michael Curtis

Being Present in Pastoral Ministry

Michael is assistant dean of residential life at Gordon College in Wenham, Massachusetts.

It is easy to go through our day with countless conversations and interactions with coworkers, clients, family, and friends, only half-listening. We are easily distracted by deadlines, sidetracked with our own stuff, and preoccupied with that pretty, shiny phone that keeps giving you updates and notifications, and the promise that there is something more interesting than whatever or whoever is around you. Scott Gibson, however, has the gift of making you feel known, seen, accepted, and loved. He listens. Whether it is when he greets you at his door for a get-together, sees you in Starbucks, or sits with you over a meal, Scott slows things down and is present with you. He has helped teach me about the power of presence in pastoral ministry.

I am thankful for Scott, and I have learned a great deal from him during my time of being mentored by him during seminary. Internally, I felt a little on the outside, because I was one of the few students he mentored who did not feel called to preach in the local church as a lead pastor. My peers were either planning on pursuing further study or applying to serve in the local church. I knew I wanted to be involved in relational student ministry, but I was unclear where God was leading at the time. Scott never made me feel like an outsider, though. He was so welcoming and encouraging during my time of vocational discernment. The Lord clearly led my wife and me to Gordon, a Christian liberal arts college where I have served in residence life for the past ten years: first as a resident director (RD), then as the director and assistant dean of the Residence Life Program.

As an RD, you have the opportunity to literally live with the people you are ministering to. You have daily interactions, conversations, and experiences with the residents who live in your building. You lead a staff of resident advisors (RAs). And, as an RD at a Christian institution, you have the privilege of mentoring and discipling your staff of RAs. You also witness a lot of difficult life issues—students wrestling with their parents getting divorced, grieving the loss of a loved one, the ending of friendships and dating relationships. I've dealt with the death of a student in a car accident, parents committing suicide, and students recovering from trauma and abuse. While we connect students to additional resources, like our counseling center, an RD has the opportunity to remain with the student during this difficult season, to be present with them. I am so thankful for God's presence in these situations, for the encouragement and wisdom of coworkers, and for Scott's example of communicating care through listening well and prioritizing the person through walking alongside them in the midst of tragedy, confusion, frustration, and sadness. Scott has given me an example of sharing in suffering and delighting in the demonstration of God's faithfulness.

When you walk into my office, you'll see a verse on the wall. I put it there intentionally. As the assistant dean of residence life, I have the privilege of walking alongside students during seasons of joy and celebration, as well as through difficult and dark seasons: students wrestling with anxiety and depression, and students who have considered or made an attempt at taking their own life. I also have the opportunity to meet with students in discipline situations, where we navigate through regret, shame, guilt, misunderstandings, apathy, hard-heartedness, fear, and doubt. This verse serves as a reminder to all who enter—students, staff, parents, and myself—and a prayer for them, that they might experience the gift of being fully known and fully loved:

> The Lord your God is with you,
> He is mighty to save.
> He will take great delight in you,
> He will quiet you with his love,
> He will rejoice over you with singing.
> (Zephaniah 3:17, NIV, 1984)

Zephaniah is a prophetic book written to Judah, where there is a decision in front of the nation—to turn back as a nation and keep their covenant with God, or face judgment. The book is a warning against judgment coming in the day of the Lord, and seeks to awaken repentance and the possibility of forgiveness, restoration, and blessing from God. Zephaniah 3:17 comes from the end of the book, where there is the anticipation of hope in Judah's return and God's promised restoration. It's in that hope, in that restoration, that we can see a glimpse into who God is and how he views us as his beloved children.

This verse is important to me because it reminds us that the Lord our God is with us, that he is literally in our midst. Living on this side of salvation history, we understand that the Word became flesh and dwelt among us through Jesus, our Savior, Emmanuel, who is God with us. After Jesus ascended to the Father, he sent the Holy Spirit to dwell in us and among us. We serve a God who is mighty, great, and glorious, and who dwells with us. If that were not enough, we learn that God delights in us, quiets us with his love, and rejoices over us with singing.

Pastoral ministry gives us the opportunity to be present with our people: to see them (really, truly see them) by listening well, knowing some of their stories, and sharing the good news of God's delight in them, and the promise of his continued presence with them. God does not simply tolerate the people he has entrusted to us. He delights in them, rejoices over them, and loves them with an everlasting love. When our people experience failure, and feel ashamed, guilty, or condemned, we can encourage them to draw

Part Five: Pastoral Ministry

near to God, to let God lift their heads, and to remind them that he delights in them.

God also knows you as a leader—all the junk, all the failures, all the sins, and he still loves you. God offers forgiveness in Christ and views you through the lens of the sacrifice of his Son. You are fully known and fully loved. As you engage in pastoral ministry and share in the burdens of your people—all of your worry, anxiety, and stress, let God quiet you with his love. Let him bring peace, stillness, quiet, and rest to you. Listen to the song he is singing over you; not a song of condemnation, but rather a beautiful song of redemption and of delight. As you sit with your people and minister to them, slow things down like Scott. Communicate care by being present, and remember that God is present with you.

Paul A. Hoffman

The Fundamentals of Pastoral Ministry

Paul is lead pastor of Evangelical Friends Church in Newport, Rhode Island.

"If God calls you to be a missionary, don't stoop to be a king."
—Jordan Grooms[1]

Recently, a pastor friend referenced the quotation above, but substituted "pastor" for "missionary." Immediately a pang of chagrin hit me. I have served as a pastor for over thirteen years, and in my humble opinion, ministry is alternately glamorous and grimy, distinguished and draining. "Actually, being a king sounds great sometimes. Who will coronate me?" I thought to myself.

I imagine Titus felt the same way quite frequently. He was appointed as pastoral overseer, tasked with organizing new churches on the notorious island of Crete. Cretans had a reputation for being "always liars, evil brutes, lazy gluttons."[2] Given these challenges, the Apostle Paul penned a letter to his protégé, Titus, instructing him how to execute his pastoral calling in this hostile environment. Of particular interest here is Titus 2:11–15. This is a salient

1. Hattaway, *Asian Harvest*, 55.
2. Titus 1:12b.

text for at least three reasons: 1) It is one of Scott Gibson's favorites; 2) it provides a clear précis of the gospel; and 3) it establishes the kind of one-on-one pastoral mentoring Scott Gibson has faithfully embodied in his life and ministry.

Perhaps most importantly (given our present purpose), Titus 2:11–15 answers the question, "what does a pastor fundamentally do?" We receive an answer via four, active imperatives. First, Titus 2:15 commands pastors to "teach" parishioners the gospel, defined as "the grace of God that brings salvation . . . [expressed in] our great God and Savior, Jesus Christ, who gave himself for us to redeem us from all wickedness and to purify for himself a people that are his very own."[3] Foremost, pastoral ministry is proclaiming the gospel. On many occasions, Scott has implored me to "preach the word and take people deep." Teaching is not primarily about entertainment or being relevant or amassing a crowd or ego gratification (the preacher's or the audience's). Instead, our teaching must "show integrity, seriousness and soundness of speech."[4] Why? The gospel is the story of God, and its message has endured over two millennia—it has preceded us and will outlast us. It is eternally significant, and individually and socially transformative. Only the gospel can make liars honest; only the gospel can make evil people good; only the gospel can make the lazy hardworking; and only the gospel can make the gluttonous generous. Pastors teach the gospel.

Secondly, pastoral ministry involves incessant encouraging. At various seasons in my ministry, I felt exhausted and despondent, due to betrayal or frustration. During these times, I fled to Dr. Gibson seeking comfort, reassurance, and inspiration. He never failed to deliver through words of prayer and affirmation. Likewise, pastors encourage their flocks by injecting courage into the weak and weary. The best way to do this is by lifting up their heads and re-fixing their gaze upon Jesus Christ, our never-failing good Shepherd. Consequently, pastors would do well to remind

---

3. Titus 2:11, 13–14.
4. Titus 2:7b–8a.

themselves that their authority to encourage comes from Jesus and is focused on Jesus.[5] Pastors teach the gospel and encourage.

Thirdly, pastors will rebuke sinful behavior and attitudes because the gospel demands it: "It teaches us to say 'No' to ungodliness and worldly passions, and to live self-controlled, upright and godly lives."[6] In the original language "rebuke" means to "bring to light, expose . . . convict or convince . . . reprove, correct."[7] While many pastors dislike (abhor?) confrontation, it is necessary to keeping the congregation healthy and holy. At times, the pastor must speak the truth in love and tell people what they don't want to hear: that it is discordant with Scripture and thus sinful to marry a non-Christian, watch pornography, divorce your spouse for selfish reasons, verbally abuse your wife or husband, spread gossip, and so on. True ministers will not shirk this duty. Yet, they engage in these hard conversations with humility and genuine sadness, having removed the "plank" from their own eye beforehand.[8] To his credit, Scott Gibson has modeled this command and lovingly corrected friends, family, mentees, students, and coworkers when their gospel witness went askew. Indeed, pastors teach the gospel, encourage, and rebuke.

Lastly, according to the Apostle Paul in Titus 2:15, pastors must refuse to be despised (disregarded) by anyone. Jesus Christ has authorized their ministry regardless of their age, sex, race, education, etc. This does not make pastors superior to other humans; but it means they are called and sent by the triune God to proclaim, guard, and embody the good news of Jesus Christ—crucified and risen. Consequently, we must not allow rebellious schemers to undermine or oppose orthodox gospel ministry. Following Paul's instruction to Titus, Scott has insisted to me and to others that we stand up to church bullies. We are to kindly but firmly confront those who would seek to commandeer the church according to

---

5. "Encourage and rebuke with all authority"; see Titus 2:15.
6. Titus 2:12.
7. *Elegchó*; Arndt and Gingrich, *Greek-English Lexicon*, 249.
8. Matt 7:3–5.

PART FIVE: PASTORAL MINISTRY

their personal agendas. Pastors teach the gospel, encourage, rebuke, and refuse to be despised.

To summarize, Titus 2:11–15 indicates that pastors teach the gospel, encourage, rebuke, and refuse to be despised. While this description does not encapsulate the full scope of the pastoral vocation, ministry is no less than these four, core activities.

I am grateful to God for providing Titus 2:11–15. I am also thankful to Scott Gibson for faithfully and fruitfully living out this text in our day. His example is worth respecting and emulating.

Dana J. Smith

Pastoral Ministry
The Steadying Influence of a Godly Mentor

Dana is senior pastor of Immanuel Church in
Chelmsford, Massachusetts.

This one pushed me to the breaking point, or so it seemed. My body was shaking, my thoughts were racing, and my stress, had I some gauge with which to measure it, would have surely been in the danger zone. It was the first year of my time as the senior pastor of a healthy, evangelical church outside of Boston. I was about to turn forty, but felt as if I was aging incrementally with each passing day.

A well-respected person in the church had just admitted to me that he had inappropriately touched a minor, and as a mandated reporter in the Commonwealth of Massachusetts, I had to act on this information. The authorities were notified, setting the legal process in motion, and my church, except for the elders, could not know a thing for the better part of a year until charges were officially brought against the congregant.

We had the proper legal counsel as a church, said what we could once the charges went public, dotted our I's and crossed our T's. However, the heartache would not leave me. How do you balance ministry to a congregant and his or her family with one of the historic marks of the Church: church discipline? How do you minister to a victim, especially when the victim was never a part of your church? On a personal level, how do you shut off your mind at night so you can be present for your own family and also get the proper rest needed for effective ministry?

Wave After Wave

While the above story was the first wave crashing onto my ministerial shore, it certainly was not the last. From staff conflicts, to married couples in various stages of marital distress, to people in the church involved in the occult, to instances of domestic violence amongst the people of God, the waves seemed more often than not to be a near constant barrage of sinful practices, each crashing onto the shore of my office. God was not holding back as the Holy Spirit was churning up problem after problem from which people needed to repent, and in the midst of which they needed godly, biblical counsel. Spend any time in vocational ministry and you will quickly have your ego crushed (and that's a good thing!). You will feel your own ineptitude in the face of heavy life situations. And if you are not careful, you too will be crushed under the weight of ministry.

Coffee, Long Discussions, and the Words "I Love You, Brother"

Scott Gibson long ago ceased being Dr. Scott Gibson to me. Truth be told, I never had him as a professor. So while I knew of him in that capacity, my relationship with him did not take shape until years after I graduated from seminary. Having recently moved back to the Boston area and serving, at the time, in the same denomination as Scott, I asked him to moderate my Ordination Council. From that time on, the friendship has grown deep and wide. He's a Western Pennsylvanian, while I'm from Eastern Pennsylvania, so we share Pennsylvanian culture (sort of). What really connects us is the fact that neither of us is a New Englander. The first thing you have to learn when ministering in New England is that, unless you are born here, you will never be considered a New Englander. You are tolerated, to be sure, even accepted, but you're always an outsider. Scott and I smile and accept our roles and our callings, often doing so over a cup or two of coffee, perhaps with a gluten-free Rice Krispie treat to top it off if we're really ready to let loose.

Scott's counsel and friendship over the years has been immeasurable and much appreciated—to say the least. The Lord has provided this mentor to me to serve as a steadying force in the midst of ministry's crashing waves. You see, Scott is not only a professor, but he also understands the world of the pastor, because he has not only been a pastor, but from time to time he continues to serve as an interim pastor. As such, I know that when I come to him to pour out my feelings, my convictions, my doubts, my joys, and my sorrows, he understands.

This gentle man patiently listens, offers a timely corrective (when needed), smiles, empathizes, and promises to pray for me. He continually encourages me to preach and to teach the word rightly, to minister biblically, and to shepherd with love and conviction. When the time comes to call it a day, my dear friend puts on his hat, opens his arms wide, gives me a strong, assuring hug, looks me in the eye, and says, "I love you, brother."

For those of you with a mentor in your life, you know how important such a person is. For those of you seeking a mentor, be diligent and keep pursuing someone, particularly someone who has more experience than you and can be the voice of reason, either to talk you off the ledge in your *I-have-to-be-the-worst-pastor-ever!* moments or to take your superhero cape off in your *How-did-this-church-exist-all-these-years-without-me?* moments—whatever the case may be. Finally, for those who think they can go it alone, trusting only in the enabling power of God, might I encourage you to remain faithful in your dependence upon our triune God, while reminding you as a brother and fellow minister that God often empowers and enables us to serve in the ministry through the counsel, wisdom, and encouragement of fellow ministers.

For every Timothy among us, may the Lord graciously raise up a Paul. And when the Lord opens the door, may we, with much humility, seek to be a Paul to the next generation of Timothys.

Part Six

Preaching

Kerry L. Bender

Congregational Intent
The Questions of Your Congregation Are More Biblical Than You Think

Kerry is currently a PhD student at the London School of Theology in conjunction with the A. J. Gordon Preaching Guild at Gordon-Conwell Theological Seminary.

CHRISTIAN HISTORY, THEOLOGY, AND art have given us no shortage of memorable images for the preaching task. In my mind's eye, I can see John Stott building his bridge, spanning the gap between two worlds.[1] Martin Luther provided an almost grotesque image of the preaching task from the position of the listeners when he suggested that, in order to see Jesus, Christians should pluck out their eyes and place them in their ears.[2] Matthias Grünewald depicted the task of the preacher by giving the elongated finger of John the Baptist pointing to the crucified Jesus in his painting of the Isenheim altarpiece. Grünewald's pictorial representation of the preaching task inspired Karl Barth's theology of proclamation, and Barth in turn provides several images of the preacher and

---

1. John Stott's *Between Two Worlds* continues to be an influential preaching text, and has shaped how many see the preacher and preaching.
2. Pelikan, *Luther's Works*, 224.

preaching: the herald, the marksman, and the preacher holding the newspaper in one hand and a Bible in the other.[3]

Of all the images of preaching that have captured my imagination and informed my preaching, however, the most profound for me is the cheek of my professor and mentor, Dr. Scott Gibson, pressed tightly against his open Bible. Whenever we, as students of preaching, would stray from the biblical text in our discussion of the "big idea" of the sermon, Scott would quickly pick up his Bible, open it, and press his cheek tightly against its pages, reminding his students that the commission and content of the preaching task finds its origins in the pages of Scripture.

Of course, postmodernity, reader-response criticism, and a hermeneutic of suspicion have raised serious questions concerning the ability of the reader, interpreter, and preacher of Scripture to actually know the intent of the author's words, much less encapsulate them again in the words of a sermon for the modern listener. How can the preacher keep her cheek pressed tightly against the text when she cannot be certain of Paul's or Moses' intentions because these documents were written long ago in what can feel like a galaxy far, far away?

This is an important question that cannot be trivialized nor handled completely here. It has been discussed, however, in detail by others.[4] While much has been written about authorial intent, one area that seems to be underrepresented in this discussion is "congregational intent." By this, I mean the following: what is the intention of the questions that are raised in Scripture by those who are first confronted with God's self-revelation? In other words, what is the intention of the questions of the Bible's first congregations in both testaments?

---

3. The image of Barth preaching with a newspaper in one hand and the Bible in the other is more legend than fact; he did make a variety of statements, however, regarding the importance of reading the newspaper and the Bible, and allowing the Bible to interpret the newspaper. This is most clearly seen in a *Time Magazine* interview from 1968. See "Barth in Retirement," http://content.time.com/time/subscriber/article/0,33009,896838,00.html.

4. For an excellent evangelical response to reader-response criticism, see Vanhoozer's book, *Is There a Meaning in This Text?*

While it is true that even the questions that are presented in Scripture are presented by the author, they do provide a window into the minds and hearts of those who were first coming into contact with God's revelation of himself. By examining these questions, both explicit and implicit, it is possible to point us towards the meaning and the intention of the text as a whole. In other words, by spending more time with the questions of the text, the answers expressed in Scripture begin to take on greater clarity; or, by struggling with the "congregational intent," the authorial intent is brought into greater focus.

As preachers, we have been convinced that our job is to drag an ancient text, kicking and screaming, into the contemporary world to answer the questions we are convinced have never been faced by humanity before 10:00 AM on the Sunday morning we are preaching. The hubris of modernity, that we have questions so important that they never before have been conceived, mixed with the suspicion of postmodernity, that the answers are impossible to find, have left us either bewildered or arrogant, lost or dogmatic, legalistic or licentious, and for many of us all of the above all at the same time.

While it is true that Scripture is not a list of answers to modern questions, in reality, the questions of the twenty-first century CE are not all that different from the questions of the first century CE, or for that matter the twenty-first century BCE. The congregation of God continues to struggle with how to reflect the image of God, how to care for creation, how to keep our brothers and sisters, how to determine who is my neighbor, how to meet God in "the least of these," and what it means to live physically in one nation when our citizenship is in another kingdom. The questions that confront us in Scripture go on and on. These so-called ancient questions are echoed in our contemporary congregation and our broader culture in thousands of ways—creation care, social justice, immigration reform, racism, nationalism, abortion, human trafficking, etc. The job of the preacher is to hear the echoes of humanity's questions in the text of Scripture, as well as to see how the cross and resurrection of Jesus Christ answer these questions yesterday, today, and tomorrow.

The cheek of the preacher, therefore, must be pressed tightly against the text of Scripture—not simply because the commission and content of the sermon comes from the text, but because the very questions of this age, and every age, that give rise to the necessity of preaching in the contemporary world are found in Scripture. In other words, Scripture contains not only the most important answers, but the most important questions, not only the scratch but the itch itself. May each preacher, and each reader of Scripture, heed the advice of Scott Gibson to keep our cheeks pressed in close to the pages of Scripture.

Grant Buchholtz

Missional Preaching

Grant is the founder and pastor of Tokyo Life Church
and a missionary in Japan with the Evangelical
Covenant Church.

"Thank you. Your message was so clear and easy to understand." I heard this comment from an older Japanese woman after my first message in Japanese. Isn't this what we want as we preach? Clarity and being understood? Ultimately, we desire to see lives changed through the Holy Spirit, but it begins with a clear message that engages our listeners. The truth is that my message was easy to understand because my vocabulary was severely limited. I only knew one way to express a particular idea!

Living in Tokyo and planting a church has forced me to rethink my preaching. Our church is about half Japanese and half internationals who come from over a dozen nations and six continents. I can't simply preach a message that would work in America. I have to rethink my illustrations and what will connect. I must consider this diverse audience. Above all, I must think about how to communicate the gospel in a land where only 1 percent is Christian. Whatever your context, it is critical that mission drives your preaching, as you seek to connect people to God. Missional preaching is more than preaching on mission-themed passages like the Great Commission (Matt 28:19–20) or Isaiah's

Call ("Here am I, send me" [Isa 6:8]). Why do we preach? Who is our audience? These are critical questions to consider if we are to preach missionally.

Rooted in God's Mission

Emil Brunner states, "The church exists by mission, just as a fire exists by burning. Where there is no mission, there is no church."[1] Without mission, what are we doing in the pulpit? We are fueled to connect people to God and to pursue his purposes. We don't speak just to entertain or inform, but to make disciples who follow Jesus. Mission should be the foundation for our preaching. Then, discipleship is the goal.

Connect, Then Draw to the Gospel

Effective preaching is not just being faithful to the text, but also connecting the message with the hearers. A key question to ask is, "Who is my audience?" Compare the messages of Peter at Pentecost in Acts 2 and Paul on Mars Hill in Acts 17. They were aware of their listeners. We must meet people where they are by considering their questions, struggles, and views. What might it communicate to my Japanese listeners if every story and illustration came from American pop culture and American sports? Donald Sunukjian recommends the Life-Situation Grid to imagine your audience in terms of gender, marital status, age, and levels of faith. Imagine where the biblical truth shows up in their lives. How can it be relevant to the range of listeners?[2]

---

1. Brunner, *Word and the World*, 108.
2. Sunukjian, *Invitation to Biblical Preaching*, 112.

Preach to Those You Seek to Reach, Not Just to Those You Have

If a visitor came to your worship service, would they feel welcome or out of place? Is your message accessible for those who don't have deep biblical knowledge or hold your same views? Being missional requires us to continue being outward-focused. The way you talk not only communicates to your guests, but it also builds trust with your congregation. They know it's safe to bring their unbelieving friends to hear a message which might draw them closer to Christ. When we discuss tough issues, will your guests at least feel that you understand their position and articulate it in an honest and respectful manner? We can't persuade if we don't take seriously our listeners' norms, values, and traditions.[3]

God's heart is for your community. The cross will be offensive to some. But, we should strive to remove any unnecessary barriers that keep people from hearing the gospel. Do you only see your members? Or do you have the eyes to see your diverse community that are in need of the life-transforming and hope-giving message of Jesus?

Engage the Whole Person

Your message should not only appeal to their ears or mind, but also engage their whole person. If we are serious about God's mission, then we should passionately seek to do whatever it takes for our audience to experience the message. Instead of just delivering a logical monologue, are there ways to engage their senses? Michael Duduit notes, "Preaching attempts to not only be heard but felt, seen, and experienced."[4] Tell a story. Use visuals. Incorporate a memorable tactile object. Add an element of participation. Tie the sermon into the overall service. As individuals have different learning styles, find various ways to engage them through your message.

---

3. Theissen, *Sign Language of Faith*, 113.
4. Duduit, "Seeing the Truth," 6, 14.

PART SIX: PREACHING

Guard against cultural or intellectual imperialism. Preaching has the power to honor or marginalize the listeners. Do you pull all your illustrations from primarily male-dominated stories? I remember sitting with my wife when the speaker shared example after example from sports or from the military. While they made his point to me, they were much less meaningful for my wife. As a pastor of a very diverse congregation, my sensitivity to the ethnicity and gender of my people ascribes them value and affirms that they are welcome among the congregation. My awareness of Japanese culture, novels, and current news builds bridges with the people I seek to reach. Listeners desire examples and illustrations of life as they experience it.[5] To truly see your congregation will take work. To build bridges will require intentional thought. My default is to draw from my own memories, culture, and interests. However, this breaks down if it takes five minutes to set up an illustration from a Hollywood film, because I have to explain the plot, characters, and scene. Your message has the best chance of being heard and received when your listeners sense that you understand them and care for them. Empathy is a critical component as you recognize and value your unique listeners.

Preaching weighs two critical components: being as faithful as possible to the biblical passage and its context, while seeking to connect this message to your hearers. To do only one well is a disservice to both God and to the church.

"Preaching is discipleship."[6] May your messages be missional as they draw people closer to Christ and further in their faith.

---

5. Tisdale, *Preaching as Local Theology*, 127.
6. Gibson, *Preaching with a Plan*, 17.

Eric Dokken

Do What You Want
Getting to the Heart of Application

Eric is the pastor of Grace Community Church in Marblehead, Massachusetts.

"THERE IS A WORD that you repeated several times in the second half of your sermon: 'should.'" I had just preached a wedding sermon in a "Preaching for Special Occasions" class, and the professor, Scott Gibson, was giving me feedback. He was giving instruction I had heard him give several times before but had failed to heed. His sage advice was, "Instead of telling your listeners what they should do, tell them what they want to do."

I was a single seminarian exhorting a hypothetical bride and groom to practice the virtues listed in Colossians 3:12–17 in their marriage: "You should love one another, you must forgive each other, etc." I had little idea what that would look like in a marriage, and this couple had an even smaller probability of putting it into practice just because a preacher said they should. Who remembers what is said in their wedding sermon, let alone puts it into practice?

For our congregation sitting in the pew on a Sunday morning, there is more hope that they will remember (and possibly even apply) some of what we say in a sermon. However, the reality is that a great deal of what is said from the pulpit is ignored, particularly the application. So, is there anything we can do to make our homiletical application more effective?

Gibson's feedback to my wedding sermon is the best advice I know to make application more effective—appeal to the listeners' desires. Rather than approaching application through duty or guilt, get to the heart of the listeners and address their sanctified motivations. Preachers can approach application in a way that listeners are more likely to respond by appealing to their desires.

The alternative to appealing to desire—and the default for many preachers—is legalistic or moralistic application. This approach appeals to duty and obligation, and is identified by consistent use of the words "should," "must," and "ought." It is true that there are a lot of things we should do as followers of Christ. It is also true that we consistently fall short of doing those things. Listeners who get a constant diet of being told what they should do may be inspired for a time, but will mostly end up with a sense of guilt. Guilt motivates for only a short time. Preachers who want to be effective will not rely on the negative motivation of guilt, but on the positive motivation of desire.

It is easy to see why preachers tend to appeal to guilt and obligation. The Bible appears to do the same thing in many places. However, a careful reading of any passage in its context will reveal that biblical imperatives are preceded by divine indicatives. The biblical motivation for obedience is ultimately not obligation, but gratitude. My wedding sermon on Colossians 3 would have been a lot stronger if I had tapped into the indicative/imperative structure of Colossians. Paul spent two chapters exalting the person and work of Christ, the image of the invisible God, before exhorting his readers to live as people who are dearly loved. Those who are dearly loved don't forgive and love because they have to, but because they want to.

Jesus uses positive motivation in the Sermon on the Mount; which, ironically, is sometimes dismissed as a legalistic sermon. In the sermon, Jesus calls his followers to a standard of righteousness beyond what is seen in the law-obsessed Pharisees. Anyone who thinks that they can or will achieve that kind of perfect life is delusional. Jesus' goal is not to have his listeners walk away thinking that, if they work harder, they can earn their way into the kingdom of heaven. Rather, he wants his listeners to realize they are incapable of living up to the perfect standard of righteousness.

Humbled by our sin, we hear the good news of the first beatitude, the beginning of the Sermon on the Mount: "Blessed are the poor in spirit, for theirs is the kingdom of heaven."[1] In recognizing our spiritual bankruptcy, we mourn our poverty before a holy God. Knowing we have nothing to offer God, we can now receive the gift of the kingdom from the one who perfectly fulfilled the law. This gift from Christ is the deep desire of every true follower, as Jesus tells us in the fourth beatitude: "Blessed are those who hunger and thirst for righteousness, for they shall be satisfied."[2] The message of the Sermon on the Mount is that Jesus has fulfilled the heart of the law so that his followers can now do what they long to do: fulfill the law from the heart. Effective application appeals to that spiritual appetite, the desires of the heart.

Listeners are not often aware of their deeper appetites and desires. A good sermon introduction that effectively raises a need enables listeners to recognize what is in their heart. Effective application presents the fulfillment of these desires. Gibson says this approach to preaching elicits a "'yes yes' response from your listeners."[3] They agree with the application rather than resist it, because the preacher has helped them recognize that it satisfies a need that they have. The application tells them what they want to do, even if they didn't realize that's what they wanted before the sermon started.

Application that appeals to desire will elicit a response far beyond obligation-driven appeals. In his sermon against "practical moralism" titled "The Expulsive Power of a New Affection," Thomas Chalmers says that a man will set his property on fire out of obligation "with sore and painful reluctance." However, "if he

---

1. Matt 5:3 (ESV).
2. Matt 5:6 (ESV).
3. Gibson, "Mood Isn't Always Imperative," 2:20.

saw that a new property of tenfold value was instantly to emerge from the wreck of the old one," he would eagerly light the match.[4] Likewise, Jesus exhorts the crowds in the Sermon on the Mount to pluck out their eyes and saw off their arms. While not intended to be taken literally, Jesus is calling for radical obedience which no one would do out of a mere sense of duty. The only hope to elicit that kind of devotion is to appeal to desire, which is exactly what Jesus had done in the fourth beatitude. Preaching that taps into these deep desires will draw a congregation into far more dramatic deeds of obedience than simply telling them what they should do.

Effective application will not aim to burden listeners with a sense of obligation, but will instead cultivate the deepest desires of the heart, the desire for righteousness. This approach is the best way to produce long-term obedience in our congregations. Saint Augustine said in his sermon on 1 John 4, "Once for all, then, a short precept is given thee: Love, and do what thou wilt."[5] If your heart is full of love for God and for others, your actions will be loving because that is what you want to do. As God cultivates love in the hearts of our listeners, we can encourage our congregation to do whatever they want.

---

4. Chalmers, "Expulsive Power," 305.
5. Saint Augustine, "Homilies," 866.

Nicholas Gatzke

Discipling to the Task of Preaching

Nicholas is senior pastor of Old North Church in Canfield, Ohio, and visiting lecturer of preaching at Gordon-Conwell Theological Seminary.

WHEN A PERSON DISCIPLES young preachers, he does something that will bear fruit long after he is gone, and the benefit for the kingdom of God will only be fully realized in eternity. It is with this long view that Scott Gibson has approached the discipling of preachers, and he has given others, including myself, this same vision.

There are many important aspects to discipling preachers. Below is one practice and one value that Scott Gibson has displayed over the years. They may not be the most important of all the values and practices, but they have proven to be incredibly valuable to me and are very helpful in raising up the next generation of preachers.

The Practice of Honest Critique

It is a difficult thing to give helpful feedback on a sermon for a variety of reasons. When a person writes a sermon, it becomes a part of him. The faithful preacher will pour over the biblical text for hours, carefully craft a structure, and adopt specific words and phrases to try to convey his ideas, and then he will bathe it in prayer, pleading with the Father to glorify the Son through the ministry of the Spirit. When the preacher delivers a sermon, there is a wonderful mental and emotional release that occurs. The word of the Lord has been building up within the preacher to a point where he cannot hold it in any longer. He must proclaim it to the congregation, and when he does, he is excited and relieved to do so. The sermon has become a part of the preacher, as he has formed it, and it has formed him. Now, upon delivery, it has become a part of the community.

At this point, the preacher longs for positive feedback and encouraging words. As one can imagine, it becomes difficult to give constructive critique, because it can often be perceived that to critique the sermon—the sermon that has become a part of someone—is to critique the preacher himself. Consequently, many avoid giving helpful critique, or soften the content of such analysis out of a desire to not hurt or offend the preacher. However, when discipling preachers, constructive critique—given at the right time and in the interest of the preacher and the congregation—is exactly what the preacher needs in order to improve. His ability to receive this critique will in many ways inform his suitability to the long-term nature of the task.

Critique is very simply a careful analysis of the many facets of the sermon with the goal of helping one improve. The most helpful types of critique are those which are direct in their encouragements and direct in their warm but constructive criticism. When a young preacher has someone in his life who knows the important elements of the sermon; understands the propensities of the preacher; and walks alongside him, guiding, directing, and speaking the truth in love, this can change the trajectory of a pulpit ministry. This is what honest critique provides, and it is an invaluable practice to give and to receive.

The Value of Biblical Faithfulness and Rhetoric Together

There is a growing divide within evangelicalism regarding the practice of preaching. On one side, there are some who promote expository preaching as the most faithful type of preaching, while dismissing the importance of the persuasive tools of sermon delivery. On the other side, there are those who promote a more personality-driven type of preaching that significantly moves the emotions of the congregation and persuades them to the preacher's point of view. This preaching is often described as "passionate," "filled with vision," and engages people with the things of "real life." Sadly, some of this preaching minimally engages the biblical text, rarely preaches through entire books of the Bible, and regularly seeks to pull spiritual principles out of the text without engaging the greater theological purpose or relationship to the gospel that the biblical author seeks to communicate.

An important aspect of mentoring preachers is to help them see and demonstrate the value of faithfulness to the biblical text that works in concert with the rhetorical devices of the sermon. The two poles described above need not be in competition with each other. It is a false dichotomy to believe that a sermon can only contain one or the other. That being said, it is important to note the order of priority of the two and how one actually functions in the service of the other.

If preaching is a Jesus-commanded and Spirit-empowered work, then the preacher must pursue faithfulness to communicate the whole counsel of God in a detailed fashion, as it is presented in Scripture. Laziness in engaging the Bible or placing the content of the Bible in a subservient role to the ideas or personality of the preacher by simply brushing up against it in the sermon is actually a form of unfaithfulness to the task. As a preacher continues to mature, he grows in confidence that the Spirit of God will accomplish the work of God through the proclamation of the word of God. Faithfulness to proclaim the word becomes the standard for success, and this success is most often achieved through a steady diet of expository sermons.

Preaching not only engages the head and the heart, but also the emotions of the hearers. The use of rhetorical tools aids in this engagement. Specific attention to sermon form, structure, illustrations, vocal tools, and how the preacher communicates through his personality all serve to engage the congregation and can be helpful in persuading them to the point of the text. Held in their proper position, faithfulness to elucidating the main idea of the biblical text along with passionate, persuasive delivery can work together to create a powerful sermon.

The written works and the discipling relationships that Scott Gibson has invested in have displayed this practice of healthy critique and have promoted the value of biblical faithfulness and rhetoric together. May the Lord be glorified and the kingdom expanded as more preachers are trained for this great task of preaching.

Part Seven

Teaching and Academics

Patricia Batten

A Teacher of Teachers

Patricia is ranked adjunct assistant professor of preaching at Gordon-Conwell Theological Seminary.

My first crack at teaching homiletics came because of Scott Gibson. He was granted a one-semester sabbatical and needed someone to teach his homiletics courses while he was away. Yes, Scott brought a woman into the preaching department. A big idea woman, of course.

Scott, you see, is a central idea fanatic. That's no exaggeration. He teaches the "big idea" with excellence. He is clear. He is purposeful. He is truly a central idea fanatic.

But before he ever brought me on board, he made sure I hadn't jumped the big idea ship for calmer seas. After seminary, was I still committed to central idea preaching? If not, I would surely be walking the preaching plank.

I remember the first time Scott checked in on me in my ministry context. Unannounced, he and Rhonda strode into the sanctuary of my little ABCUSA church in Kennebunkport, Maine, one Sunday. Scott and Rhonda made conversation easily. They mingled with the flannel-clad hunters and shook the coarse hand of our salty lobsterman. They thanked Naomi for the sharply creased bulletin she folded that morning. They politely accepted an unusually thick slice of cheddar cheese from the aged hand of Helen, the church cheese-slicer and coffee-maker.

It was December and the pulpit platform had been transformed into the village of Bethlehem, the house of bread. I was dressed in the garb of an ancient Judean woman, kneading dough and wondering if the bread of life had really come to the house of bread.

At the end of the worship service, Scott thanked me for preaching a "clear, central idea sermon." He was beaming, but denied me his trademark hug because I was covered in flour (Scott suffers from celiac disease). I was his student, and I was doing my best to put into practice all that he had taught me. My attempt certainly wasn't perfect, but I took it seriously and I worked at it.

I understand now that there is no greater joy as a teacher than to see your students practicing what you've taught them. More than a final exam or any other tool of assessment, you know that learning actually took place when you see that understanding has been transferred to an actual ministry context. Educators Wiggins and McTighe call this transferability: "Understanding is about transfer.... To be truly able requires the ability to transfer what we have learned to new and sometimes confusing settings. The ability to transfer our knowledge and skill effectively involves the capacity to take what we know and use it creatively, flexibly, fluently, in different settings or problems, on our own."[1]

Scott is a teacher par excellence.

Fast-forward a couple of years. I've passed Scott's "big idea" test and now he's preparing me to teach his classes for one semester. This preparation began with the thump of an enormous three-ring binder on his desk. The impact was so intense that it sent shock waves into his office, stirring the stacks of paper on the floor and causing a tremor in his candy dish. The M&M's rattled. I did too.

Scott gave me his preaching notes. This was a big deal in the world of academia in 2007. Professors aren't known for their skill in sharing, but Scott is not afraid of collaboration. He expected his colleagues in homiletics to make the central idea central in their

---

1. Wiggins and McTighe, *Understanding by Design*, 40.

classrooms. He was more than willing to contribute his expertise and his experience to make sure the central idea was central at Gordon-Conwell. Our department is stronger because of his commitment to expository preaching. He is a teacher of teachers.

Academia can sometimes be marked by a rugged independence with little collaboration. But Scott's desire was that our department be on the same page when it came to teaching about preaching. Yes, we all have our own teaching styles, but we had better be teaching central idea; we had better know the organic and the developmental questions; and we had better know how to outline a sermon. Scott is a teacher of teachers.

His notes were stored in tattered binders with current illustrations and articles stuffed into plastic pockets. He went over every single lecture with me. We sat down together for several weeks and reviewed those notes in detail. I raided the candy dish. He complained that he needed a new system of organization. He gave me the preaching final exam. Let me be clearer. He made me take the preaching final exam during one of our prep sessions. He watched as I wrote. No pressure. More candy. Scott is a teacher of teachers.

Scott has often reminded me that preaching is a skills-based course. We are teaching our students how to preach central idea sermons. As a result of taking the course "Preaching: Principles and Practice," a student will be able to preach a central idea sermon.

But Scott also knows that ministers are involved in more than sermon-making. They visit the sick and encourage the homesick. They study the Bible and teach Bible studies. They are disciple-makers and, when necessary, status quo shakers. We are teaching students to preach sermons to flesh-and-blood people: the young, the old, the rich, the poor, the educated, the uneducated, the sinner, the saint, the girls, and the boys.

Pastors don't just preach sermons. They preach sermons to real, live congregations.

That's what makes Scott the best of teachers; a teacher par excellence. As a pastor, he preached sermons to real, live people; people he knew and loved and shepherded. He visited the sick and encouraged the homesick. He studied the Bible and taught Bible studies. He was a disciple-maker and a status quo shaker.

He has always been a champion of me, my preaching, and my teaching of preaching. I'm grateful to him for his support and continued encouragement in my teaching endeavor. Scott is a teacher par excellence.

CALVIN W. CHOI

Scott Gibson, the Teacher

Calvin is the senior pastor of Watertown Evangelical Church in Watertown, Massachusetts, and an adjunct professor of preaching at Gordon-Conwell Theological Seminary.

FEW STUDENTS GET TO know their teacher in various capacities: as a teacher, a research tutor, a doctoral advisor, a counselor, a mentor, a friend, and a colleague. I am one of those few who've known Scott M. Gibson in all those capacities for the last twelve years.

Once a preaching professor told me, "Calvin, preaching professors have to be good teachers, good sermon evaluators, and good preachers." Then he added, "And I rarely meet someone who is good at all three." But in response to his comment, I remember thinking to myself, "But I think I know who is good at all three."

In 2008, the A. J. Gordon Guild, a joint PhD program in homiletics, was established between Gordon-Conwell Theological Seminary and London School of Theology in England. Since he was aware of my keen interest in pursuing a doctorate in preaching, Scott strongly encouraged me to enroll in the program. He became my doctoral supervisor. Our tutoring sessions often began with a cup of tea and biscuits. He was masterful at critiquing, challenging, and encouraging me. He knew when to pull and push his students. One day, he walked into my research office and found me writing. In his pleasant tone he said, "Calvin, I am glad to see you at your desk. Remember, you write your thesis with your butt, not your head." I laughed because I knew exactly what he meant. After three years of toil and tears, I became the first graduate of the PhD program. Over the years, he not only shaped me to love preaching but also made me love teaching about preaching. Much can be said about his commitment and love for teaching about preaching and pursuing excellence in preaching, but here are four thoughts that have stuck with me over the years.

To Scott, teaching about preaching is not just informational, but relational. He understood that teaching about preaching was more than a classroom activity and transfer of knowledge, but it must be accommodated by a genuine interest in building relationships with students. He found creative ways to engage with his students. He made every effort to get to know me as much as allowing me to get to know him. One of his preaching courses that impressed me during my ThM year at Gordon-Conwell was having his students over for a dinner prepared by him and his wife, Rhonda (an exceptional host), followed by a living room discussion on the subject of preaching. He regularly invited his students for a meal because he believed in the power of breaking bread. He understood that teaching about preaching is more than just getting to know students' names and grading their sermons.

To Scott, teaching about preaching is not just a technique or a method, but it must be grounded in sound theology. He is a "big idea" preacher, and he is not shy to tell others about it. He not only believes in it, but he is consistently good at it. This is why he devotes a chapter of his book *Preaching with a Plan* to the practical theology of preaching.

To Scott, teaching about preaching is not just sermon evaluation, but it is also discipleship. Some students think and know that they are "good" preachers, and sometimes such pride can rub off on the teacher. He told me once about a student, "He thinks he preaches well and he does. But he has to learn to be humble." He understood that teaching about preaching is more than sermon evaluation and assigning grades. It is discipleship.[1]

To Scott, pursing excellence in preaching and teaching requires critical thinking, reading, and writing. He taught me how to think, read, and write critically. He always tried to create a critical learning environment. Every Friday, his doctoral students held a roundtable luncheon with the late Dr. Haddon Robinson. We would make brief presentations on various topics in preaching, and we would discuss and critique books, articles, and theories of preaching. His scholarly mind is what had influenced me the most as a lifelong learner of preaching.

He believes that teaching about preaching must be practically relevant, theologically sound, and academically refining. That has been his aspiration ever since he founded the Evangelical Homiletics Society in 1997. Teaching about preaching should never be divorced from cultivating and promoting scholarly discussion and research.

He loves preaching not just in words, but also in actions. He does everything he can to promote the cause of preaching inside and outside of the classroom as well as in his writings. Preaching, teaching about preaching, and pursuing excellence in preaching have been the thrust and priorities of his life.

He once said smilingly, "Calvin, I know there are many preachers better than me, but there is only one Scott Gibson." With his wit and humility, he always knows where he stands in the world of homiletics. He refuses to take pride over others when he knows that he could. He refuses to look down on those who take advantage of him. And I am blessed to have met the one who has shown me that teaching about preaching and pursuing homiletical scholarship are not merely about acquiring homiletical skills and accolades. His genuine interest in others, unrelenting pursuit of sound theology, and using resources inside and outside of his classroom as a means of discipleship have enabled him over the years to teach well, preach well, evaluate well, and (I might add) disciple well with a scholarly mind and with humility.

1. Gibson, *Preaching with a Plan*, 17.

Part Seven: Teaching and Academics

And as much as other boys and I attempt to pay tribute to his impact on our lives, I think I know what he will say in return: "Boys, it's not about me. It's all about God."

Chris Rappazini

Mentoring Millennials and Other Young Whippersnappers

Chris is a professor/minister and a millennial who has a passion for preaching that takes Scripture seriously and works hard to make it applicable to everyday life.

IN FULL TRANSPARENCY, DURING my first several years teaching in higher education, I was in over my head. As a faculty member who was also a millennial, I had more in common with the students than I did with my colleagues. I also quickly discovered that I was hired to teach but expected to do much more. My coworkers and administers were swift to assist, when needed, but there is part of a young faculty member that does not want to reveal one's desperation. In the midst of drowning in a sea of faculty and committee meetings, advising students, navigating school politics, speaking in chapels, guest lecturing, publishing, working on new course prep, and grading, grading, and more grading, I needed someone outside of my institution to disclose the real truth that I needed help.

I am tremendously and eternally grateful that I could pick up the phone and call my mentor, Scott Gibson. I probably called him every other week for the first couple years as I tried to get my instructor legs under me. I honestly do not know how I could have made it without his guidance. For those mentoring someone from a younger generation in the area of teaching, academics, or really any related field, I suggest three components of mentoring and discipleship that Scott Gibson did for me that were tremendously helpful: listening, counseling, and giving loving encouragement.

Listening

Contrary to popular belief, millennials crave wisdom and advice from those with more experience. However, before receiving instruction, millennials want to be heard first. I recognize that this is selfish, but we want to know that someone cares about us. In a society where everyone is talking, millennials have a deep desire to be heard and understood. The best thing that Scott did for me was to be quick to listen and slow to speak (Jas 1:19).

There were times throughout the academic year when I needed to express my frustrations and vent or verbally process about a situation. In retrospect, it was vital that I had someone who would listen and ask open-ended questions. However, for many—myself included—we tend to be quick to speak and distracted while listening. But I suggest having a listening-first disposition. According to Larry Spears, listening is the overwhelmingly top characteristic of servant-leadership.[1] Listening is crucial in any relationship, especially when mentoring someone. If Scott would not have taken the time to listen first, I do not know if I would have been able to receive the wise counsel that followed.

Counseling

Please do not equate counseling with lecturing. Nobody likes to be lectured, especially by a mentor. For most millennials, it brings back bad childhood memories of finger-waving parents or school teachers. There is a place and time for lecturing, but not necessarily in a mentor/mentee relationship. Counseling can take many

---

1. Spears, "Character and Servant Leadership," 25–30.

forms, and I am so thankful that Scott never lectured me, but instead counseled me.

I am not an experienced counselor, nor do I claim to know much in the field, but I do know what worked for me as a millennial. After spending a significant amount of time listening to my situations and asking inquisitive questions, Scott would often guide me and coach me through different scenarios. Occasionally he would share helpful, personal stories from his own experiences that would shed light on my circumstances. Even after the phone call ended, Scott continued to counsel me through regularly sending me articles and books that pertained to our conversation.[2] This was extremely helpful, because it often spoke directly to my situation, but more so, it demonstrated that Scott genuinely cared about me.

Loving Encouragement

The most important aspect of Scott's mentorship has been his ability to listen and give wise counsel out of a heart of love. Scott exemplifies what it means to speak the truth in love (Eph 4:15), and there was never any doubt that he believed in me. As a millennial and junior faculty member, doubt has a way of creeping into one's mindset. Self-confidence can quickly erode with one bad student review, and self-esteem can diminish after a faculty meeting. Loving and encouraging words can make all the difference. I would regularly get emails, texts, and handwritten cards from Scott reminding me of his unending support and God's calling on my life. Many of those cards still hang on my bulletin board as a constant reminder of his love and encouragement. Young men and women need to know that someone like you believes in them and genuinely wants them to succeed. Your words of loving encouragement will go a lot further than you think.

As a young homiletician in the academic world, Scott has always treated me with the utmost respect, given me the reassurance

---

2. Burge, *Mapping Your Academic Career.*

I needed, and inspired me to achieve things I never imagined. He is dependable, trustworthy, and loyal. Whenever I need advice on teaching or in my personal life, he is always quick to listen and give wise counsel. Like Haddon Robinson, Don Sunukjian, and other pillars in evangelical homiletics, Scott has equipped and deployed thousands of great preachers. His passion for making disciples of the next generation is second to none, and I hope you and I can follow in his footsteps.

ALLEN YEH

Advice for Applying for Grad School in Theology

Allen is associate professor of Intercultural Studies and Missiology at Biola University near Los Angeles, California, and the author of *Polycentric Missiology*.

LIKE DR. SCOTT GIBSON, I am an American who did his DPhil in theology at the University of Oxford—I credit Scott as my number one inspiration for doing so. He was not only a spiritual mentor to me, but also an academic one. He honed my thinking in the classroom at Gordon-Conwell Theological Seminary, encouraged me to do further studies in the UK, impressed me in how he strove and overcame challenges, and set my imagination ablaze by regaling me with his overseas stories. Not only did I follow in Scott's footsteps to the same university, but I also focused on a historical missionary figure who was from the Baptist tradition (he with A. J. Gordon and I with Orlando Costas). Scott taught me perseverance, raised the bar of academic excellence, and slingshot me in the direction that I am today. Truly, without him, I don't know what my academic journey would have looked like today, but it certainly would not have been as rich. I never imagined that I would end up studying in Oxford's hallowed halls, and the doors that would open for me as a result.

PART SEVEN: TEACHING AND ACADEMICS

Britain and America have often been called "two countries divided by a common language." I want to focus on Britain's educational system in this chapter, and how it differs from the American system. Oxford University is the oldest university in the United Kingdom. The exact date of its founding has been lost in the mists of time; however, most people place it at AD 1167 with the establishment of its first royal charter. Some say AD 1096, when there was certainly teaching occurring in its hallowed halls. Regardless of which date is chosen, Oxford is indisputably the oldest university in the English-speaking world.

Despite the fact that American universities (e.g., members of the Ivy League like Harvard, Yale, and Princeton) clearly came later, sometimes the influence has gone the other way. Yale actually invented the PhD, which spread to other American universities, and British/European universities emulated their younger counterparts across the ocean. Think about the Inklings, like C. S. Lewis and J. R. R. Tolkien: they all taught at Oxford with "only" a master's degree, no doctorates. That was the norm until the American influence swept through.

The main questions I want to address here are: Should you do a PhD in theology or some kind of Christian studies? And if so, should you do it in Britain or in America?

Should you do a PhD?

First of all, think carefully whether you want to do a PhD. It is potentially 3–7 years of your life where you intensively study one tiny microscopic topic in exhaustive detail. Do you have that kind of personality and perseverance? I know some people go to law school because they don't know what else to do with their life and it helps to "stall" (while doing something that looks impressive) while they get their bearings and discern the next steps. Do not do this with a PhD—if you are not passionate about what you are studying, you will burn out. If you are not committed to the fullest, you will give up. If you are not hell-bent on becoming a professor, then go for a different degree. Even if you can answer in the affirmative to all of the above, everyone who does a PhD—at some point in the course of their degree—asks themselves, "Why am I doing this? I want to give up." That is normal, even for the most committed people, so do not start down this road unless you are absolutely sure you want to do it; otherwise you will find yourself in a lot of debt for something you don't really care about.

The Difference between British and American Degrees

British degrees are much shorter than American ones. Three years for an undergraduate degree as opposed to four. One year for a masters instead of two. Three years for a PhD instead of seven. An American PhD in theology will require you to learn French and German (even if they have nothing to do with your thesis topic), take two years of classes before even starting your dissertation, take a series of comprehensive exams, T. A. classes, and then when you are ABD ("All But Dissertation"), then you can finally work on that major piece of writing. In Britain, you start off your degree as ABD! You can start writing that dissertation the day you start your program.

Why You Should Not Get a British Degree

Depends how much you want independence (and no, I did not mean that as a pun)! Someone once likened a British degree to being parachuted into the middle of a dark forest and you're expected to find your way out. If you want guidance, do an American PhD. Your British supervisor will not be of much assistance. You may enjoy the fact that the British PhD is shorter, but if you can't be independently motivated, it would be better to do the American degree, which has more regulations and more hoops to jump through, but guides you through the process step-by-step.

Why You Should Get a British Degree

International Exposure

You become a much better "world" scholar, and not just a parochial American scholar. That being said, unfortunately your international perspective is not very quantifiable, so even though it makes you a well-rounded person, it doesn't necessarily help your CV.

Freedom and Independence

You can run on your own without having your supervisor hold your hand all the way or keep you on a short leash.

The Ability to Write as a Christian

Even though Britain is only nominally Christian, they have no separation of church and state, so everyone still thinks of themselves as Christian. Therefore, you can write a Christian dissertation from a faith perspective without getting your hand slapped. It's much harder to get away with that in an American secular university.

Advice for Finishing your Dissertation

My DPhil (that's what they call a PhD in Oxford, but it's the same thing—Doctor of Philosophy) supervisor gave me two wise words of advice: 1) Your dissertation is not your magnum opus. It is a credential for joining the guild of scholars, similar to how a lawyer needs to pass their bar exam. Just get the thing done so that you can join the academy, and then write your magnum opus later. Your dissertation is your first attempt at a major piece of research, and nobody gets it perfect the first time. Remember this is simply your freshman attempt. I certainly hope that your later writings are better than your first piece of writing, not the other way around! 2) There are two kinds of dissertations: the perfect dissertation; and the finished dissertation. Again, just get it done.

I hope this insider information helps in guiding you toward a potential PhD and whether or not you go the British or American route.

Part Eight

Wisdom

Thomas F. Backer

Pastoral Wisdom

Thomas is an ACPE certified educator and board-certified chaplain in Omaha, Nebraska.

IT WOULD SEEM THAT wisdom for ministry is in precious short supply these days, in spite of the voluminous amount of seminars, webinars, podcasts, books, and journals pumping out statistics, strategies, and steps to successful ministry. What appears less available in the American pastorate today is wisdom for ministry. Many commentators would suggest that a contributing factor to this decline in wisdom is the lack of mentors available to pastors, especially young pastors starting out in ministry. Others might suggest that young leaders often overestimate their capacity for leadership and do not see the need for mentors.

Scott Gibson has dedicated a significant percentage of his ministry to mentoring young pastors. He has seen the need and has made a commitment to mentoring those called to pastoral ministry. His mentoring often takes the shape of offering wise counsel in the midst of a confusing time. I am in the third decade of pastoral ministry, and I am still being mentored by this unique man who is a pastor, scholar, preacher, collaborator, confidant, colleague, and friend. It is with gratitude that I offer this reflection on wisdom in ministry.

Part Eight: Wisdom

Wisdom is that quality of thoughtfulness that helps the perplexed make decisions. Wisdom knows that beyond a particular decision—or rather, one might say, behind the decision—are multiple perspectives that frame the decision in different ways. These perspectives account for the complexities inherent in the decision in different ways. Wisdom is the quality of discernment that chooses a perspective which accounts for the most salient factor in the situation requiring a decision.

A less desirable outcome in a ministry situation is often the result of an inexperienced pastor making a decision without an awareness that there are multiple perspectives which can illuminate the nature of the decision at hand. It is not that wise pastors possess crystal-ball accuracy in discerning the one and only choice among competing choices. Rather, pastors rely on a wisdom that refuses pat answers and the party line. Wisdom steps back and tries to understand the situation before making a decision.

Wisdom is not only about perspective. It is about timing. Wisdom resists the tendency to rush to judgment, especially common in young pastors facing difficult decisions for the first time in their ministries. Wisdom sees beyond the moment and is often content to let things play out before changing direction. Wisdom is like the running back who waits for his blockers to get out ahead of him before hitting the hole. Great runners wait for the play to come to them rather than trying to force it. A really great runner is sometimes described as possessing the quality of being a patient runner. Similarly, wise people pay attention to design, timing, and opportunity. In many ways, pastoral wisdom—the wisdom that pastors need for fruitful ministry—is no different than the wisdom needed by any leader. Pastoral wisdom includes dimensions of perspective and patience. But it is more than that. Pastoral wisdom is a textured knowledge that comes from maturation and experience in ministry, success and failure, bended knees and dog-eared Bibles—and from listening and speaking. Pastoral wisdom is the uncanny ability to know the difference between what is permanent and what is passing. I would suggest that there is a quality in pastoral wisdom that recognizes moral and ethical dimensions of situations that confront pastors as well.

More than any other quality, pastoral wisdom contains an awareness of God in the midst of mundane and momentous decisions. Pastoral wisdom dwarfs cleverness. It recognizes that God is present and available to those seeking wisdom. Mentors remind pastors of this reality. This is a welcome relief to the overachieving pastor who thinks that he or she should be Solomon-like in their decisions. Mentors remind pastors that it is God who calls and who equips those who are called.

Mentors like Scott help the young leader learn that ministry is not about him or her, which is so prevalent in the narcissism of new pastors raised in a culture of entitlement and celebrity. Scott reminds the minister that discipleship does not stop at graduation or ordination. God is always seeking to train and teach pastors. Ongoing discipleship is not optional in ministry. Pastoral wisdom does not avoid the demands of discipleship that face the pastor before he or she ever steps foot in the pulpit or prays with a parishioner. I have seen this in Scott's life, and he has shared the challenges of his own ongoing discipleship in the church and in the academy.

Scott Gibson demonstrates what pastoral wisdom looks like for those who seek counsel for life and ministry. Scott is the kind of man you want on your speed dial. I have sought his counsel countless times since graduating from Gordon-Conwell. When I was flustered by a colleague's ego, disturbed by what I realized what was lurking in my heart, floundering in marriage, discerning a change in ministry focus, and preaching in unusual circumstances—Scott was there on the other end of the phone or replied to an email. The wisdom that Scott shares from his heart is what James describes as considerate, impartial, and sincere.

There are so many things that distract pastors today. Politics, polls, and pet peeves can move us off center. We can be petty and popularity-minded. Our spiritual disciplines can slide and our words can start to sound and feel empty. We can pout like Jonah or run away like Isaiah. We can hide like Peter. But someone like Scott can see that in our lives and call us back to the ministry that

PART EIGHT: WISDOM

God gives us. If we seek it, we can find deep wells of pastoral wisdom to bring us back to the center—deep wells that bring us back to Jesus and the call to follow him, and to bear witness to what he has accomplished and what he is building in our time.

John Q. Dao

Well-Versed in Wisdom

John serves as a social worker near Boston, Massachusetts.

"Do you have a life verse, John?"

Admittedly the question caught me a little off guard. We had just finished our regular Tuesday dinner together, and had retired upstairs to two leather recliners in a small room just across from Dr. Gibson's home office.

"A what?" I stammered, as if I've never heard of the concept before. The truth is, in my eight years of being a Christian, I had never once considered a life verse as something I needed and was a bit embarrassed that I did not have one.

Dr. Gibson sat across from me, reclined all the way back in his chair with his feet extending well past the footrest capped with a lovely pair of house slippers. In his lap sat a small Bichon Frise laying with her head nestled between his legs.

"A life verse. I have one. Do you want to know what it is?"

I nodded my head in earnest.

"Luke 2:52. 'And Jesus grew in wisdom and stature, and in favor with God and man.'"

The answer wasn't what I was expecting, but then again, I never quite knew what to expect when we entered that small room together. Picking up on my curiosity, Scott continued, "You see, Jesus wasn't born knowing everything, but he had to learn just like we do. Throughout his life, he continued to grow in wisdom, in stature, and in favor with God and with man, and is an example to me that we are never finished in our own growing."

We ended the night in typical fashion, sharing life's updates, and lifting one another up in prayer. Although I didn't leave that night with a life verse of my own, I did leave with a sense of wonder and contemplation.

It's only in looking back now that I realize that there was nothing random about that night. There are many knowledgeable teachers out there, men and women with lived experiences and stories that carry so much weight that you feel their presence as they walk into the room. And although Scott doesn't know everything, he knew me. He knew how, week after week, I would come to him with a new problem in my life weighing me down. He knew how I was being pulled in multiple directions in trying to save a failing relationship, a sinking academic career, and questions about faith and sexuality. He had the wisdom to see my lack of direction when I was blind to it.

From that wisdom came a plan, and from that plan a single question:

"Do you have a life verse, John?"

It connected with my heart. It stopped me in my tracks to pause and think, and in that moment (unbeknownst to me) I too grew in wisdom.

If I had any advice to give to those seeking to mentor others, it might be something you'd hear in Dr. Gibson's first preaching class: "Know your listeners. Where do you want them to go? What do you want them to learn or see? How do you want them to change as a result of this?" Truth be told, I don't know how much preparation Scott puts into each of our meetings, but each one felt intentional, carefully crafted, and prayerfully guided. Mostly. Sometimes we just ate Kirkland vanilla ice cream, and he would tease me for liking Turkey Hill vanilla ice cream better. That's important, too.

Chad D. Granger

The Fear of the Lord is the Beginning of Wisdom and True Fear of the Lord Comes through Discipleship

Chad is assistant pastor of Urban Hope Community Church in Fairfield, Alabama.

> The fear of the Lord is the beginning of wisdom,
> And the knowledge of the Holy One is insight.
> —Proverbs 9:10 (ESV)

Growing up in the heart of the Bible Belt in a Christian home and attending church every Sunday, I thought for most of my life that I feared the Lord. I prayed the sinner's prayer at eight years of age at church camp and rededicated my life at every church camp after that. Now, as I look back over my adolescent years and into college, I feared my parents, I feared death, and I feared hell, but I did not truly fear the Lord. Of course, I always gave a respectful nod to God as a good Southerner by attending church, blessing my meals, and saying my prayers at night, but I think it was more of a cultural reflex than an intimate relationship. I knew a lot about the Holy One, but I did not truly know him. God and his word were not authoritative in my life. I was my own master.

Part Eight: Wisdom

It was not until my senior year of college that I truly began to fear the Lord. After mastering my own way for twenty-two years and trying to find life through feasting on the fleshly desires of the frat dream, I hit rock bottom. I was depressed, empty, and hopeless. On the bedroom floor of my trailer in brokenness and in humility, I called out to God. It was an honest cry of desperation; a wrestling for insight, understanding, and purpose. It was repentance. I finally understood why I needed the Christ I had heard about my whole life. In the midst of tears and snot, God with abundant grace and mercy answered me. An authentic faith and fear in the Lord began to bud.

Although I do believe true faith and fear in the Lord began that night, it was not an overnight transformation. The clouds did not part. I was not struck by immediate insight. But what God did in that season was to send God-fearing men into my life who had a high view of his Scripture. For the first time in my life, I started to be discipled, and God's word started to come to life like never before. What once seemed dry and confusing started to become sweet and clear. A Christ who seemed foreign and distant became near and dear. As insight came through the guidance of the Holy Spirit and through mentors, so did a new desire for obedience. God and his word became authoritative in my life. Authentic fear in the Lord began to flesh itself out in wise living and in the fruit thereof.

In book of Proverbs we learn that "the fear of the Lord is the beginning of wisdom" (9:10; 1:7, ESV). Fear of the Lord is not a mere emotion; it is a lifestyle of reverence through desired obedience to God and his word. Wisdom is not mere knowledge; it is rightly applied knowledge to life in accordance to God's word. All true wisdom comes from God, but God often chooses to use the ordinary means of discipleship to bring forth his wisdom. Fear of the Lord is modeled by God-fearing men and women living out the word of God and inviting others into their life to do likewise alongside them through intentional discipleship.

If I have gained any wisdom in my short three-and-a-half decades of life, it is due to God graciously and faithfully putting God-fearing men in life wherever he has taken me. These men have invited me into their lives and been spiritual fathers to me in the Christian pilgrimage. They have taken me under their wings and have taught me and instructed me through word and action how to walk and live wisely in fear of the Lord. All of these men have revered God and his word, and have lived out wisdom alongside me.

It is my great privilege to say that one of these spiritual fathers that God brought into my life during seminary is Dr. Scott Gibson. For six months before making the journey from Alabama to Massachusetts, I prayed for God to provide a new mentor. And he did so abundantly with this great man. Dr. Gibson was much more than just my preaching professor; he was a weekly life confidant of biblical wisdom. Over cups of Dunkin' Donuts coffee and North Shore beachscapes, I poured out my anxieties about graduate school, marriage, and ministry call before him. He listened to me. He laughed with me. He cried with me. He prayed with me. He comforted me and counseled me with the care of a friend and of a father.

Dr. Gibson's discipleship was the epitome of an invitation into life. He hosted me for meals and hired me for snow shoveling and house projects. He graciously knew I needed the money, but I was also convinced that he was preparing me for a backup career if he was unable to teach me how to clearly preach the big idea of the passage. Thankfully his professorial instruction was as thorough as his discipleship was intentional. He made time for me, and I am wiser now than when I first wandered into his office. It is my aim to honor him and all my spiritual fathers by carrying on their legacy of passing on the wisdom of the fear of the Lord and knowledge of the Holy One, and by inviting others into my life through intentional discipleship.

Todd Regester

Wisdom
The Right Path

Todd serves as a spiritual care coordinator for McLaren Hospice and a chaplain/firefighter near Flint, Michigan.

OUR FRIEND AND MENTOR Scott Gibson directed a week of summer camp in 1987. As a counselor and would-be pastor, I was impressed by his ability to guide and to inspire. While our roles and hairlines have certainly changed over the years, the goal has always been to positively influence lives for Christ. In this, he has ever been our champion of wisdom.

Wisdom is not a matter of intelligence, book learning, or native ability to grasp a concept. Wisdom arrives when we practice the truth. It is a God-given practical "know-how" that abides when it's followed. It is God-ordained. It is relational.

Wisdom is revealed.[1] James encourages us to confidently ask the Lord, who gives without finding fault, for wisdom.[2] Wisdom is foremost God's truth, and we are usually too full of our own delusions and deceptions to pursue it honestly and submissively. It must break through our natural ignorance and pride.

1. Prov 2:6; Job 28:20, 23.
2. Jas 1:5.

For this reason, wisdom is both positional and relational. It is positional in that it is received through humility and correction. David, in Psalm 51, isn't really in recovery until he acknowledges both God's authority to judge and to align with his will.[3] The perfect gift of right perspective is from God, not from us, but we must seek it. Consider by contrast a fool who is thwarted by his supposed superiority.[4]

Inasmuch as wisdom is revealed through position, God designed it to be learned in relationship. Isn't it easy to grasp God's fatherly heart through the words of Solomon? We hear a father's loving plea to look and listen for wisdom, to understand the fear of the Lord.[5] "Keep to the path, don't stray!" he warns.[6] "Hold on to instruction, do not let it go; guard it well, for it is your life."[7] God's loving-kindness directs us to a better path.

We need people to show us the way. Out of appreciation for my mentor Scott, I carved him a walking stick with the text from Proverbs 13:20: "Walk with the wise and become wise." We don't learn something so relational as wisdom in a vacuum. Think of how you have gained valuable life skills or perspective. I'd bet there is a person's name nearby.

At this point, we remember Wisdom personified. The example of Jesus stands starkly against the world.[8] In Christ, John says, is no darkness at all. In fact, it is his perfect example that shouts out our need for forgiveness and purity.[9] The words and actions of the Master are the focus of every true disciple. The righteous path is his, after all.

Having said that, reflected light still reveals. Other shepherds may assist the Great Shepherd, and other servants still assist the

---

3. Prov 51:4.
4. Prov 1:7.
5. Prov 2:4–5.
6. Prov 1:8 (my paraphrase).
7. Prov 4:13.
8. 1 John 2:15–17.
9. 1 John 1:5; John 1:1–14.

PART EIGHT: WISDOM

Servant of all. Many pastors and teachers have lost real fellowship with the Master by neglecting any substantial fellowship with his body. The church points to the path of Christ.

Not only is wisdom caught and taught, illustrated and modeled, but truth learned in context is truth understood. It must be sought. We don't readily understand love, perseverance, and hope without practical experience. While my father might model right-living, he cannot live my life for me. Solomon or not, most fathers of teenagers quickly realize that we can only guide our children so far. We may not walk alone, but we must each choose to walk.

Greater wisdom is won through honest living. We discover through struggle and failure, along with fearless examination. Is it a coincidence that the belt of truth leads our adornment of the armor of God? Regular self-searching, openness to Spirit-led appraisal and approval are integral. Having discovered the path, we must keep to it. It leads to righteousness and godliness.

Wisdom is perhaps a straight path, but it is not simple. It is comprehensive. I love the admonishment in Proverbs 4:23 where it says, "Above all, guard your heart, since everything you do flows from it." The following verses address our lips, eyes, and feet: what we say, see, and do. We must be all in. In living this out, we must be people of principle, based on Scripture. To call ourselves loving, we should approximate Jesus' example of patience, kindness, humility, sacrifice, temperament, truth-telling, and so on.[10] As we study the word, know it, and keep it, we find God's approval.[11]

We must also be people of the Spirit, faithful to Christ's example, and guided by his hand. If the fear of God is the beginning of wisdom, how may we approach everyday situations with a sensitivity to the Almighty? How can we understand the greater context, a higher perspective, or the biggest benefit without him? Should we speak or be silent? Act or not act? When we walk God's path, we listen again and again for his voice.

Having said all this, let's give God thanks. How marvelous the path and those who follow! How beautiful the life of Jesus, as seen

10. 1 Cor 13:4–7.
11. 2 Tim 2:15.

in Scripture, and the testimony of ongoing disciples who make disciples. How amazing that we share the journey together at this moment. Pray that we grasp the sacred brevity of life, numbering our days that we might have a heart for wisdom![12]

---

12. Ps 90:12.

Todd M. Smedley

Wisdom's Pedagogy
Humility

Todd is the senior pastor of Fourth Presbyterian Church in Bethesda, Maryland.

WEDNESDAYS WERE MY NIGHT to have dinner with Scott. It was a ritual that I looked forward to every week and one that we rarely missed. The three-hour time of fellowship took on its own ritualistic pattern; a sort of rhythm that became habitual but not tiring. Normally I'd request the same meal: "Jacko Chicken," Scott's culinary invention. The meal would be ready upon my arrival. Conversation would flow naturally and organically during the meal with an ease that is hard to describe. Then came the cleaning ritual. He would wash; I would dry and put away the dishes. Then we would move to the living room for more talking and conclude with prayer for each other. There was a wonderfully familiar and comfortable liturgy about the whole evening—one that would cause anyone to open one's soul to another. I suspect every other brother discipled by Scott had a similar, if not identical, experience.

The regular practice, like washing and drying dishes side-by-side, as we did, serves as an illustration for how we should seek to teach wisdom to those whose lives we are called to influence. You cannot, or at least should not, teach wisdom to others directly or didactically. Wisdom does not come through the front door, but through the back door. Much like humility, the moment we perceive our own wisdom we flaunt our folly. Similarly, when we come to the task of mentoring others from the perspective that we have the wisdom they need, we can be sure they will not gain much. They will soon tire of us and be no better off for having been with us. You could tell Scott's subconscious mentality was never, "Oh, I have much to teach you," but rather it was "Would you like to learn and grow alongside me?" "Do not be wise in your own eyes" (Prov 3:7a) is the necessary posture for discipling others. Mentors are merely senior learners.

Wisdom is not something we can instill in our own lives, let alone in the lives of others, by way of direct teaching or specific guidelines. There is no program of discipleship or step-by-step process to lead others to wise living. To use the cliché, we might say that wisdom is "caught, not taught." It is more likely to be learned as we work and pray side-by-side with those we mentor. Francis Bacon is attributed as saying, "He that gives good advice, builds with one hand; he that gives good counsel and example, builds with both." Scott built into my life with both hands.

I cannot remember any occasion when it felt as if my mentor was teaching me how to be wise. My guess is that he was not conscious of it either, which is probably why Scott was so effective in encouraging me to "gain a heart of wisdom." It is only in hindsight, as I reflect on his influence in my life, that I comprehend how truly wise his mentoring approach was and is. But it was not particular things he said or did that left this lasting impact on me. In fact, I do not remember very many specific nuggets of wisdom that I have taken from Scott and tucked away in my ministry tool chest. It was from being immersed in life with him, week in and week out, that I was winsomely and imperceptibly shown what it was to fear the Lord. It was the whole package, his life selflessly offered to me, which made me so willing and able to open mine to him.

For example, how did one who is fluent in a different language come to learn this new tongue? It is unlikely they remember any single lesson or particular assignment in their arduous pursuit of learning the language, but it is each unmemorable class or daily exposure to it that cumulatively led to fluency in a language not their own. Similarly, the pursuit of wisdom is a cumulative and arduous task. It does not come naturally to sinners, and few are fluent in it; but walking with the wise, who know not their wisdom, has transformative power.

Wisdom comes by being immersed in formative practices and rituals, much like the rituals Scott and I practiced together every Wednesday evening during my time at seminary. It is indiscernibly and unconsciously gained over the course of years of listening, learning, praying, and sharing life with people wiser than yourself. Since it does not come through the front door but slips in through the back door, wise people are the last to discover that they have learned wisdom.

In a word, wisdom's pedagogical method is humility. The paradox in awakening wisdom in another is the recognition of one's own insufficiency. Proverbs 11:2 reminds us that "When pride comes, then comes disgrace, but with humility comes wisdom." The genius of Scott's way of mentoring younger brothers in the Lord is his humility—his self-forgetfulness. I suspect that is why so many men have been drawn to and impacted by the man we honor in this book. It is only appropriate that we honor him, for wisdom tells us that "humility comes before honor" (Prov 15:33).

Stephen Sebastian

Afterword
Living a Life of Mentoring Influence

Stephen is a general dentist in the US Army who served as a pastor for over eight years and now resides in Pinehurst, North Carolina.

Where does a book on mentoring leave us? Where do we go from here?

The previous chapters speak of the power mentoring holds to influence a person's life. Mentors shape and mold us, encourage us, and challenge us. They influence us to be better, stronger Christians. Our hope is that these reflections on mentoring will motivate you to seek the influence of mentors in your own life, and to be that influence for others.

How do we do it? There's no program we need other than time, and no book other than the Bible. This was Scott Gibson's approach. It's simple enough for us to follow as well.

I confess I haven't been much of a mentor myself. I've done better through the years at being mentored than being the mentor. There were days when I served in the ministry when I wondered if I was having any influence at all.

But these reflections on mentoring inspire us not to give up. We resolve to be better mentors, first in our homes with our own

PART EIGHT: WISDOM

sons and daughters, and then with other Christians in the church and throughout our Christian communities. Sure, we may never become a prolific mentor like Scott. But we can strive to do what we can while leaving the results to God. Seek mentors, become mentors. In this way, we live a life of mentoring influence.

My Experience with Mentoring

My introduction to mentoring was actually in college, long before I met Scott Gibson. A campus ministry staff member climbed six flights of stairs to my dorm room every week, just to say hello and ask how he could pray for me. (His name just happened to be Scott, too!) His relentless effort to pursue me left quite an impression. I eventually accepted his invitation to meet for Bible study and for prayer.

In seminary, Scott Gibson picked up where the first Scott left off. As a first-year seminary student, I was young and eager, but undirected and lacked confidence. I knew another Christian mentor is what I needed.

Scott Gibson rented a room in seminary right across the hall from mine. As a doctoral student, he stacked his research papers carefully in tall piles on the furniture and on the floor. I walked through them like a maze one day to ask him if he would consider mentoring me. He told me to pray about it, and the next week we got together for our first meeting.

There was no program we followed or curriculum we used. Scott simply cared enough to set aside his work to spend time with me. He pointed me to the Scriptures as I shared with him my struggles. He challenged me to live more intentionally for Christ.

In later years, Scott and I would meet every Sunday evening in his apartment for a roast chicken dinner that he prepared himself. Though busy as a young professor, he seldom missed our evenings together. After dinner we'd clean up and retire to the living room where we would talk and pray. And every evening he would challenge me with direct questions:

What has God been teaching you lately?

What areas of your Christian character could you stand to improve?

Where do you see God leading you a year from now, five years from now?

What has been your greatest temptation this week?

What is it that you don't want to tell me?

These last two questions were particularly penetrating. For young single students, temptations abound. A couple years into seminary and already I had met a wonderful girl (who eventually became my wife). Scott knew the importance of keeping the relationship pure, and held me accountable for it. We would end our evening by praying for one another and asking God to make us men of Christ-like character and godly integrity.

A Pattern for Us

A mentor challenges you to look hard at your life, to hold it up against the standards of Scripture. To that end, time spent with a mentor should center around honesty, openness, confession, accountability, encouragement, spiritual challenge, and prayer.

Scott's example also teaches that quality of time usually requires quantity of time. It's hard to gain a pearl of wisdom just by scheduling a ten-minute appointment with your professor. This is where Scott excelled. He did more than just meet briefly with his students during office hours. He would open his home and spend the evening getting to know them. Students went away feeling encouraged and supported, knowing they had an advocate on their side.

This is mentoring. Knowing you're not alone in the fight. Knowing you have a friend, confidant, and an encourager who is always reminding you of and pointing you toward the greatest Friend, Confidant, and Encourager of all—Jesus Christ. A mentor is one of your greatest supporters, believing in you more than you believe in yourself. Why? Because your mentor sees the Maker behind the man or the woman, even when you can't.

Conclusion

Hospitality, intentional friendship, genuine concern for others—these are some of the lessons we learned from Scott, our mentor. We'd all do well to review them from time to time and to put them into practice. In a fast-paced, multitasking world, slowing down enough to get to know someone (let alone having a godly influence on them) takes our concerted effort and sacrifice. But living a life of mentoring influence calls us to put forth the effort.

Let these personal accounts inspire you to do it. Resolve to find those mentors or be that mentoring influence for someone else. "As iron sharpens iron, so one man [or woman] sharpens another" (Prov 27:17). Scott has been the iron in our lives. What can you do to be that iron for someone else?

Bibliography

Arndt, William F., and F. Wilbur Gingrich. *A Greek-English Lexicon of the New Testament and Other Early Christian Literature*. 2nd ed. Chicago: University of Chicago Press, 1958.
"Barth in Retirement." *Time*, May 31, 1963. http://content.time.com/time/subscriber/article/0,33009,896838,00.html.
Brown, Brené. "The Power of Vulnerability." https://www.ted.com/talks/brene_brown_on_vulnerability.
Brunner, Emil. *The Word and the World*. Reprint. Lexington: American Theological Library Association, 1965.
Burge, Gary M. *Mapping Your Academic Career: Charting the Course of a Professor's Life*. Downers Grove: InterVarsity, 2015.
Chalmers, Thomas. "The Expulsive Power of a New Affection." In *20 Centuries of Great Preaching*, vol. 3, edited by Clyde E. Fant Jr. and William M. Pinson Jr., 300–314. Waco: Word, 1976.
Chapman, Gary. *The 5 Love Languages: The Secret to Love that Lasts*. Chicago: Northfield, 2015.
Dodd, Jimmy. *Survive or Thrive: 6 Relationships Every Pastor Needs*. Colorado Springs: Cook, 2015.
Duduit, Michael. "Seeing the Truth: The Use of Visual Illustration in Preaching." Paper presented at the annual meeting of the Evangelical Homiletics Society, St. Louis, Missouri, 2005.
Gibson, Scott M. "The Mood Isn't Always Imperative." http://www.gordonconwell.edu/resources/media/50.mp3.
———. *Preaching with a Plan: Sermon Strategies for Growing Mature Believers*. Grand Rapids: Baker, 2012.
Girard, René. *Deceit, Desire, and the Novel: Self and Other in Literary Structure*. Translated by Yvonne Freccero. Baltimore: Johns Hopkins University Press, 1998.
Guthrie, George H. *2 Corinthians*. Baker Exegetical Commentary on the New Testament. Grand Rapids: Baker Academic, 2015.
Hattaway, Paul. *An Asian Harvest: An Autobiography*. Oxford, UK: Monarch, 2017.

Bibliography

Lloyd-Jones, D. Martyn. *Preaching and Preachers*. Grand Rapids: Zondervan, 2012.

McGonigal, Kelly. *The Willpower Instinct: How Self-Control Works, Why It Matters, and What You Can Do to Get More of It*. New York: Avery, 2012.

Ogden, Greg. *Discipleship Essentials: A Guide to Building Your Life in Christ*. Downers Grove: InterVarsity, 1998.

Pelikan, Jaroslav, ed. *Luther's Works, Vol. 29: Lectures on Titus, Philemon*. St. Louis: Concordia, 1968.

Saint Augustine. "Homilies on the First Epistle of John." http://www.ccel.org/ccel/schaff/npnf107.pdf.

Spears, Larry C. "Character and Servant Leadership: Ten Characteristics of Effective, Caring Leaders." *The Journal of Virtues & Leadership* 1 (2010) 25–30.

Steel, Carolyn. *Hungry City: How Food Shapes Our Lives*. London: Chatto and Windus, 2008.

Stott, John. *Between Two Worlds: The Challenge of Preaching Today*. Grand Rapids: Eerdmans, 1982.

Sunukjian, Donald. *Invitation to Biblical Preaching: Proclaiming Truth with Clarity and Relevance*. Grand Rapids: Kregel, 2007.

Theissen, Gerd. *The Sign Language of Faith*. London: SCM, 1995.

Tisdale, Leonora Tubbs. *Preaching as Local Theology and Folk Art*. Minneapolis: Fortress, 1997.

Vanhoozer, Kevin J. *Is There a Meaning in This Text? The Bible, The Reader, and The Morality of Literary Knowledge*. Grand Rapids: Zondervan, 2009.

Wiggins, Grant, and Jay McTighe. *Understanding by Design*. 2nd ed. Upper Saddle River, NJ: Pearson, 2005.

Wolterstorff, Nicholas. *Lament for a Son*. Grand Rapids: Eerdmans, 1987.

www.ingramcontent.com/pod-product-compliance
Lightning Source LLC
Chambersburg PA
CBHW071505150426
43191CB00009B/1429

9781532641855